- categories of people you can
  convince
- know the (+) message and
  relay it (about the candidate
  & his economic intentions)

- know the crazy lies/smears
  and explain why not true

★ one-on-one conversations

- do the one-on-one yourself,
but also find ways to convince
others to do the same.
- Get out the vote, for this one
occasion

> - Drive people to polls?
> - Register people ?

- Social media → respond to political
  commentary; post your own

- email responses / testimonials
- letters to editor   - call conservative
                               talk shows

Have facts that contradict
pro-Trump stuff, from
conservative sources.

Register voters
votesaveamerica.com - ck your reg.
brennancenter.org - local rules
mobilizeamerica.io - how to
volunteer for
voter reg.

Travel to battleground states for
door-to-door
Give $

Help w/ calls or texts to battleground
states

A Citizen's
Guide *to*
BEATING
Donald
TRUMP

ALSO BY DAVID PLOUFFE

The Audacity to Win: The Inside Story and Lessons of Barack Obama's Historic Victory

A Citizen's
Guide *to*
BEATING
Donald
TRUMP

★ ★ ★

DAVID PLOUFFE

VIKING

VIKING
An imprint of Penguin Random House LLC
penguinrandomhouse.com

ISBN 9781984879493 (hardcover)
ISBN 9781984879509 (ebook)

Printed in the United States of America
1   3   5   7   9   10   8   6   4   2

Designed by Amanda Dewey

For Olivia, my guide.

CONTENTS

INTRODUCTION

★ ★ ★

November 9, 2016, 2:35 a.m. Eastern Standard Time. Do you remember how you felt the moment the United States of America elected a racist, misogynist, accused sexual predator; business fraud; and obstructor of justice to represent America and you on the world stage? To the most important job in the history of the world? Of course you remember. Still feel this way? Maybe more so. So do I. This pain, and the desire not to extend it for four more years, is why I'm writing this book and why you're reading it.

Twice I've forced myself to rewind the 2016 election-night coverage by the anchors on Fox News all the way through, from the first closing of the polls in the East to the final call of Wisconsin—and therefore the election. And I've stared at the time-lapse sequence of the

New York Times election tracking needle more than once, and every single time it swings, slowly but inexorably, from blue to red. God's honest truth is that in terms of long-lasting emotional resonance, the gut punch from Trump's victory had a greater impact on me than the elation eight years earlier when Barack Obama won—and I'd worked nonstop as his campaign manager for two years.

Without a doubt, I will be proudest of that victory professionally when I finally kick the bucket, but I've never gone back and watched more than a few minutes of either its election-night footage or the reelection four years later. I do admit to enjoying occasional reruns of Karl Rove's meltdown on the Fox set in 2012, when he insisted Mitt Romney could still win Ohio after his own network had just called the Buckeye State for Obama. That still gives me a laugh—less funny is that there were few people I respected more when it came to Presidential numbers than Rove, but it shows how even experts can be seduced by the alternative reality of the Fox set.

How could anything possibly top the emotion of that unseasonably warm night in Chicago in 2008? And yet it had, and I know that many Obama alums—including our amazing volunteers, the "ordinary" voters who stood in long lines in 2008 and then again four and eight years later, the kids who were too young to vote but not too young to understand and care, and people all over the world who were studying America's revered political system in action—all of them felt the same way in 2016, and not just because we were gobsmacked by the unexpected result. Almost all veteran politicos and voters alike have been crushed by other surprise election results. But this one hit us with its own especially awful, cruel, hard-to-get-out-of-bed-the-next-day effect. And then it was still hard to get up the day after that. The year 2016 will scar us for as long as we breathe the same air that Trump befouls with his every word.

It's not that we were simply horrified by the reality show performer and his grifter family appearing on stage as America's next first family—though what a horrifying sight that was. It's not that we were petrified and panicked about what Trump would do to our economy, our planet, our alliances—though everything we feared and much more has come true. And it's not that Trump lost the popular vote by *three* million votes and somehow won the presidency. That's the way politics can break in our system. The electoral college is the only scoreboard that matters. It's how many points you score, not how many yards you gain. My advice is to just get over this inequity. Until we change the system—and I hope we do—you have to win the game as the founders designed it. Because what's the choice?

No, I suspect that this loss still cuts so deeply for so many of us because we wonder what else we could have done to prevent this historically disturbing and perhaps democracy-destroying outcome. We've all got excuses, or ways of shifting blame upward or outward. We didn't run the Clinton campaign. We didn't help prep her for the debates. We didn't counsel James Comey to throw the most overcovered nonscandal in recent American history, Hillary Clinton's emails, right back on the front pages in the closing week of the campaign. We didn't make the editorial decision at the *New York Times* to cover that bogus issue more than any policy issue or difference between the candidates

All true. But the brutal truth is that the election was decided by less than 70,000 votes in three states. And this wasn't the first time either; other elections have been decided on even smaller spreads, with huge consequences. Think about 2000, Bush versus Gore. But for 537 votes in the state of Florida, 4,424 U.S. soldiers and more than 600,000 Iraqis would not have died in Iraq, and we might have more than a flickering chance to prevent the planet from catching fire. In 1960, JFK beat Richard Nixon by grabbing the decisive state of Illinois (perhaps with more than a little "help" from his father and Mayor Richard Daley) by less than 9,000 votes out of more than 4,000,000 cast.

In presidential elections, the ballot totals seem so big—more than 130,000,000 votes cast in 2016—that you can't believe the margin of difference in an entire state might be the vote count in one large neighborhood. That is a terrifying realization—and a lesson I learned from the first campaign I worked on, a U.S. Senate Democratic primary in 1988 in Delaware, my home state. Voting took place on a Saturday in September, and our campaign was declared the winner in a big surprise on election night. Margin of victory, almost 2,800 votes. Cue the beer and cascading balloons, then sleep it off and start planning for the general election.

But on Monday morning election officials discovered a vote count error. Due to a data entry mistake, our guy had been credited with 2,828 votes in a precinct in which he'd only gotten 28. Oops, as Rick Perry would say. That error prompted a recanvass of the results to find any additional errors, and by Thursday, defeat was snatched from the jaws of victory. We lost by 71 votes. A powerful lesson learned. If any of us on staff, or even some of our most committed volunteers, had magically intuited that we'd win if we persuaded only 36 voters to change their minds, or made sure that 72 additional supporters had gotten to the polls—well, we could have done that, and we would have worked a little harder, a little smarter, dotted a few more i's and crossed a few more t's, knocked on one more door and offered one more ride.

The lesson I took forward and deployed in every subsequent campaign I worked on over two decades in politics was to assume that each one would come down to a single vote per precinct. Act like it. Work like it. Think like it. Prepare for it. Accept responsibility for it.

When I close my eyes at night, do I sometimes see the electoral college map, state by state? Yeah, I'm one of those political-numbers geeks. Not everyone is. I understand this. And I confess that this may not be the healthiest way to live—with this level of obsession—but I also contend that desperate times require desperate measures. We may survive these four years of Donald Trump with the relatively happy result that history then remembers our self-proclaimed stable genius as a one-time, one-off leader. The jury is very much out on that question. But I'm fairly certain we won't survive eight years of him or be happy with what we've become as a society if we do.

Hyperbole infects our political coverage and commentary, but I believe this statement is thoroughly warranted: November 3, 2020, may well be the most important Election Day in American history and one of our most important days, period.

I write these words in the late summer of 2019, more than a year before the general election and just as the Democrats' primary campaign kicks into high gear. I have no idea when that campaign will be effectively settled, much less who the nominee will be. I don't know how various important issues, including the economy, the tariff wars, the border wall, North Korea, Iran, and impeachment will play out over the next year. Will the Democratic nominee be up to the task of entering the Thunderdome with dumb but ferocious Donald? It's not clear yet, but it looks like some in the early field would not be up to it. That doesn't concern me here. How good a job will Trump's campaign do? We should assume at the very least a good, perhaps historic, job of getting out their vote. That concerns me a great deal, and I hope you will be concerned too, and here's why.

When this book hits stores and websites in the spring of 2020, the unwieldy group of twenty-plus initial candidates will certainly be much smaller—two or three survivors is my guess—but we may still not know the nominee. So I understand the argument that I should wait to publish until we do know the candidate. Wrong! My timing is intentional because knowing the candidate *does not matter* in terms of getting ready for the main event, the general election. And it will take time for all of us to get ready and to win.

Please, please, do not waste vital energy and time worrying about events we do not control, or spinning our wheels trying to overanalyze and bed wet about all the stuff that will happen every day before election night. There is only one fact that you need to focus on now: our candidate will be infinitely preferable to the incumbent, and electing her or him will be up to each of us. That's the big takeaway here. Even for professionals, the transition from the primary campaign (directed at the party faithful) to the general election (directed at everybody else) is difficult and takes time. For the grassroots activists—you—it's vitally necessary to start planning and working not after the last primary, not after the convention, not after the big kickoff speeches on Labor Day, but *now*. And by *now*, remember that a lot of you live in states that have already had their Democratic primaries and caucuses. The intramural part of the campaign is over.

At least sixty-five million Americans are almost certainly committed to voting against Trump. Growing that number by five to ten million is entirely in our control. We'll do it through persuading the Obama voters who voted for Trump to come back to the light, and we'll do it by persuading younger voters in particular to stick with the Democratic nominee and not throw their critical votes to third-party candidates as symbolic gestures of rebellion and blanket denunciation. We'll do it through turnout—growing the overall number of people who walk the walk and actually cast votes. Democracy isn't a metaphor or a game. This year especially it's a deadly serious test.

All of us who want a different occupant in the Oval Office need to do more than we ever imagined, and more than we have ever done before, to win this fight. I'm talking about you, my readers, not the paid campaign staff, not the candidate's family and surrogates, not the pundits or strategists. You simply have to own this idea and accept that responsibility. No pointing fingers, no assuming someone else will pick up the slack, no waiting for a nonexistent cavalry to muster on the horizon. There is only you. That's a scary thought, I know. How can one average citizen win against Trump, Javanka, Fox, Breitbart, those Russians, and billions of dollars in lies and distortions? One person can't. But when *you* become *we*, and *we* becomes *us*, millions and millions of *us*, then we have an embedded grassroots force too powerful to be denied. That's the virtuous circle in presidential campaign politics.

If I've been asked once. I've been asked a million

times by supporters of candidates whose campaigns I've managed: "What can I do?" "What *else* can I do?" The answers are what I'm going to lay out in this book. You may believe you've given your all and couldn't possibly do more. This book will serve as a checklist to test that assumption and, I hope, a quasi-mathematical proof that there is always more to do. That there has to be more.

Over the course of my career, every campaign, it seems, offered more opportunities than the previous one, mainly thanks to new technology. The year 2020 will be no different. Seize the weapons at hand! Which means, for one thing—yup, you naysayers are going to have to reactivate your Facebook and Twitter accounts. Social media can be a nightmare—soiled by trolls and hate—but it's also a powerful megaphone for average people. You don't need a big ad buy to create a big megaphone.

Of course 90 percent of the electorate votes in states that are not really competitive. They're not battlegrounds. "I live in Alabama. We're going to lose Alabama. What's the point of working here?" Or substitute California or any one of the other forty-plus noncompetitive states.

I love this question. It's one of my favorites, and the answer is one of my favorites too. Short version: we're all in this together. The nominee builds and inspires a talented and motivated staff; the staff in turn recruits, inspires, and believes in strong local volunteer leaders; staff and volunteer leaders welcome, train, listen to, and believe in volunteers—you; and you motivate, give strength to, and make the impossible seem possible for the candidate. This virtuous circle crosses state lines, and I'll show you how it happens.

And of course, doing all you can to help Democrats win up and down the ballot where you live, no matter where you live, could not be more important. Our new president will need as many allies as possible to help dig us out from the hole Trump has put America in.

This is a practical and, I hope, comprehensive guide to everything you as a deeply concerned citizen can do to elect a new president in 2020, sometimes without even leaving your house, though it's a big plus if you do get out and about. For those for whom this will be your first political rodeo—thanks and welcome aboard! You're in for a wild ride. You'll end up knowing better than me what works for you. My ideas will spark new ones of your own. And while this book is focused on the general election and defeating the sociopath currently residing at 1600 Pennsylvania Avenue, a lot of what I want to teach and encourage you to try will work in any political race, from city council member to governor. And if you're so motivated you'd be willing to pack up your bags and work full-time on the campaign? Our nominee will need designers, data scientists, software engineers, lawyers, and community organizers. Check out their job board and jump all the way in.

I'll try my best to make you confident that neither your time nor treasure will be wasted. Boots-on-the-ground campaigning like this doesn't require special knowledge or skills. It requires commitment and work. My goal here is to unlock this commitment and channel the work. I believe I know how to help potential volunteers get over their initial fears. Fears?! You bet. Knocking on that first door, having that first door slammed in your face: it's happened to all of us who have been on the political front lines, from presidents to precinct volunteers.

But aside from the occasional rude person, interacting with voters and other volunteers is a blast. You'll leave more energized than when you started.

The oft-invoked distinction between the air and the ground campaign—first employed with warfare, I suppose, then football—pertains to political campaigns as well. Airborne media messaging is a vital battleground, and it is not restricted to multi-million-dollar TV ad buys anymore. Think Facebook, Twitter, YouTube, and all the rest. The ground campaign—registration, walking through neighborhoods to get out the vote, and much more—is dear to my own heart. I guess that's pretty clear.

It's so damned important for building the virtuous circle!
I'll begin my discussion with the air campaign in order to
set up parameters for the discussion of the ground campaign that will actually win this election and send our commander in cheat back to the links.

So, are you ready?

Then let's get to work.

A Citizen's
Guide *to*
BEATING
Donald
TRUMP

OFFENSE/DEFENSE

★ ★ ★

In any political campaign, the battle of the airwaves, which now includes the phones in our pockets as much as the TVs on the walls, requires playing both offense and defense. Offense requires sharing our candidate's ideas and plans and attesting to his or her character. This must be primarily a positive message, which is what some of us wish politics were about more of the time. Defense requires calling out all the opposition's lies and attempts to sow division, exposing them for the utter bullshit they are. There's still a place for inspirational rhetoric, but this is what politics is, or seems to be, all about all too often. Especially now.

Last time around—2016—did you get out there and inform everyone you could find about Hillary Clinton's plans on taxes, community colleges, jobs and wages? Probably not, or very infrequently. I know I failed on that score. I spent all of my time and energy retweeting coverage of the latest Trump outrage. And while all this outrage certainly did motivate many of us, we did not help the candidate reach potential supporters with her economic message. And of course the press paid close to zero attention to that part of her platform, or any of it, because that's how the press rolls these days. The big three TV networks spent only thirty-two (thirty-two!) minutes on issue coverage in 2016. Press coverage of campaigns has become more Jerry Springer, less Walter Cronkite.

A good defensive campaign against lies and fabrications is necessary, and the discussion of how best to play defense follows, but we cannot let ourselves disappear down this toxic rabbit hole. We must take command of the conversation—play offense—by painting the contrast between the incumbent and our Democratic nominee, by emphasizing the positive case for our nominee, by motivating the individual voter to do just that—vote *for* something, not just *against*. I'd like to talk about the more pleasant task first.

In the Trump era, most voters are locked in, about sixty-five million of us—the number I cited in the introduction—are very unlikely to vote for the man. #NeverTrump. About sixty million are very unlikely to vote against him. The vast,

vast majority of these Trump supporters have not wavered and never will, no matter the evidence, not even if their lives have been made demonstrably worse by his actions and policies.

Clinton famously denigrated half of these folks as "deplorables." Some clearly are. But that was a lot of eggs to put in that basket, and it was self-evident enough without having to step on a political landmine to underline it. Did the comment have any effect? I haven't seen any conclusive data, but it did turn into a rallying cry that likely increased GOP enthusiasm and activism.

My point is let's not worry about people we can't convince or who fall into the trap of thinking, "How can all these people vote against their own self-interest?" Seriously, get rid of that kind of thinking. People like to define their own self-interest, not be lectured to from an ivory tower about what it should be.

Let's focus on those who are gettable. In the impending election, there will be plenty of Americans who are going to vote—we'll address those who are at risk of not voting in a later chapter. And a portion of these "definitely voting" voters are not locked in, which to us has to mean that they may vote for the Democrat. They're real, not mythical. They don't look like unicorns. They are as ordinary as the neighbor next door, and we can win some of these good people.

In 2020, they'll likely fall into the following categories:

FIRST-TIME VOTERS

Historically this cohort skews heavily Democratic, but we absolutely cannot take them for granted. Some will be undecided.

THIRD-PARTY VOTERS

A higher percentage of Clinton's voters than Trump's who were flirting with a third-party vote never came home to her, based on exit polls and other postelection research. It could have been in part because while clearly these voters did not love Clinton, they loved Trump less, but they thought she was going to win so it was OK to cast a protest vote. The votes collected by the Libertarian Party's Gary Johnson and the Green Party's Jill Stein were not an insignificant factor in her loss and may have turned the election.

That math is straightforward: Trump's ceiling was 46 percent nationally and 47 to 48 percent in key battlegrounds. He won the critical state of Wisconsin with just 47.2 percent of the vote. The two main third parties accounted for almost 6 percent of all votes cast. It was the largest percentage for third parties since the Perot years. In 2020, Trump's ceiling may still be in the same range as in 2016—not 50 percent. All of the possible third-party voters won't vote Democratic, but we need to bring on board as many of them as we can to make his win number as high as possible, and therefore not attainable.

OBAMA/TRUMP VOTERS

An unlikely sounding metamorphosis, I know, and when this species was discovered, I had a hard time believing the news—but these much-talked-about voters are alive and well, especially in Pennsylvania and the Upper Midwest. How had they preferred the young, skinny black guy with the Muslim-sounding middle name, voted for him twice, in fact, and then pulled a 180 and got down with the old racist with a gold-plated commode? I think the votes in '08 and '16 can be best explained as support for the most "changey" candidate, and the votes in '12 and '16 as support for the candidate believed to be the most authentic fighter for people like them. In '16, they were duped, obviously, and that's infuriating but also motivating: we can undupe at least some of them, maybe many.

PEOPLE WHO VOTED FOR TRUMP IN '16 BUT ARE OPEN TO AN ALTERNATIVE

Some may be voters who had deep reservations about Trump but even deeper reservations about Hillary Clinton. Or they feel that everyone has so much baggage, the corruption has been going on forever, everyone does it, my vote doesn't make any difference anyway—any number of equivocations. Still others somehow convinced themselves that Trump would drop the clown act and be more "presidential" once he got to the White House. Some might even have serious substantive problems with one or more of Trump's key initiatives, especially the tax cuts for the rich or attacks on health care. And could some have succumbed to an unacknowledged misogyny? Not impossible. It saddens me to say this, and I could be wrong, but I think there is more resistance to a woman president then there is to any male from a minority group, or a male of any sexual orientation. Hillary put cracks in the glass ceiling, but it is stubbornly strong.

VOTERS WHO DID NOT VOTE FOR TRUMP IN '16 BUT ARE OPEN TO HIM THIS TIME AROUND

Amazing but true. Sometimes these are referred to as Romney-Clinton voters, and yes, they do exist. Admittedly a small universe, this one, but there are no doubt Republican and Republican-leaning voters, many of them in suburban areas, with a higher than average income, who just couldn't pull the lever for Trump based on his appalling lack of character. They could become "transactional" voters, those who still think Trump is a personal Dumpster fire but for whom one litmus-test issue may be all that's required, and in 2020 the economy may be it for Trump. They like the tax cuts, how the economy is working for them, the rollback of many regulations. In other words, he'll have a chance to make his case to them this time. And so will we.

Much of the Democratic nominee's campaign will be spent obsessing over and communicating and measuring progress with these relatively small slivers of the electorate—in the core battleground states, just a few hundred thousand people; if the battleground map expands, a couple million. You and I need to be engaged in this arena as well.

Barack Obama was a man of high character and ethics. He had a good sense of humor. He won the "have a beer with" test in both his presidential elections. But the core of his success, especially when he won reelection with the highest unemployment rate of any president in history, was a strong sense within the middle class and among people striving to enter the middle class that no matter the color of the man's skin, his weird name, or his party affiliation, he would go to the mat for them.

Hell, he'd run through the wall for them, and he proved it with his decision to save GM and the American auto industry.

At the time, that gambit polled at 10 percent. It was a bad business idea, many thought and, surely, an even worse political one. Wrong. In 2012, the unofficial re-election slogan and rallying cry was simply "Bin Laden is dead and GM is alive." It showed up on social media, on billboards, and sides of barns in rural areas, and Vice President Joe Biden ultimately took it out on the stump. As much as everyone in the country was thrilled that the terrorist leader had been brought to ultimate justice by our Special Forces, the last part of that message was far more personal and compelling in many parts of the country, in Ohio, Michigan, and Wisconsin, for example.

In 1992, Bill Clinton's team had relentlessly focused on James Carville's mantra "It's the economy, stupid." Years later, both Obama victories were built on messages and policies aimed at convincing working-class voters that he had better solutions than his opponents. I am writing this book not knowing who the Democratic nominee will be in 2020, but as I stated in the Introduction, for the work required to uproot Donald Trump, it doesn't matter. What matters is the deep understanding that the nominee *must* win the economic argument with Donald Trump among those voters who will decide this election.

I learned all about this in the 2012 reelection campaign against the plutocrat Mitt Romney. Countless conversations throughout the country, especially in the midwestern battleground states, went something like this: "I don't agree with everything Obama has done. I wish the economy were recovering faster. But he stuck his neck out to save the auto industry. Romney would have let it die. Obama wants to cut our taxes and raise taxes on the superwealthy. Romney wants to cut taxes for people like him. And who is going to understand and fight for people like us—a corporate raider like Romney or the son of a single mom who was recently still paying off his college loans like Obama?"

That's not to say that other issues won't be important with many voters. Think health care, education, immigration, national security, lack of American prestige in the world, and climate change. They will be critically important, and the Democratic nominee needs to speak to them persuasively, but the economy will be the central front in this war. No matter what else is said and what else happens, target voters will need to see clearly that the Democratic candidate will wake up every day, take the elevator down from the White House residence, walk across the Colonnade to the West Wing, enter the Oval Office, and make decision after decision aimed at bettering their lives and the lives of their families. Unless voters feel this connection and trust in their guts, the odds that Donald Trump wins reelection will soar. If November comes and persuadable voters testify that "he drives me crazy with the tweets and I think he's a terrible person, but I think he's been OK on the economy and the Democrat wants to turn us into a socialist country," we will likely lose.

Your candidate's baggage is bigger than my candidate's baggage? For sure that's the case in this next election, but this kind of calculation will win . . . second place. Which is last place in a presidential race. Voters want to know, that is, *feel*, what the candidate stands for, not just against. The GM decision proved that President Obama, at great political risk (10 percent approval!), was willing to take on heavy political barnacles to fight for the American worker.

In 2016, Donald Trump's campaign worked relentlessly to undermine Clinton on the grounds of her assorted baggage—the emails, Benghazi, her husband, and the rest of it—but all this could only help support the orange-haired candidate's peculiar but nonetheless effective economic messaging.

The message was often dishonest and hypocritical to the point of shamelessness, but it worked. With many voters it's still working. Learn from history: Hillary Clinton and her campaign undoubtedly could have done a better job of getting across her economic arguments, and for sure they could have drawn a more effective contrast with the Republican, but the success with which Trump played the role of fearless fighter for the forgotten middle class was one of the most remarkable feats of utter bull-shit in modern American political history. If he gets away with this again . . .

"He's got my back. He has never lied to me." How many times have I read or heard this explanation from a Trump supporter? I, like you, want to yell, "He does not have your back! He has lied to you every single day. He will say anything! You know this! He has sold you down the river!" But of course, yelling out of frustration isn't the answer. We have to calmly prove that this em-peror has no hair, orange or otherwise, and we have to help the Democratic candidate make that gut connection on kitchen-table issues.

The identity and character of the Democratic candi-date will be the most important factor in closing the sale on the economy in 2020. If target voters like and trust this man or woman and have faith in their commitment to help improve their own lives, our job will surely be easier. But if we rely solely on the nominee's charisma and perfectly run campaign to get people to pull the right lever, we will, once again, come up painfully short.

We don't know what the state of the economy will be as we head into Election Day, but we do know two things. One, despite the low unemployment rate, many

Americans feel no better today than they did three years ago, much less ten years ago. Trump promised that he and he alone would change this vulnerability among "the uneducated," as he so ungraciously labeled them, but people are having to work harder than ever, stringing together multiple jobs, many part-time and without benefits, to get by, no matter how high the Dow soars. Remember, only about half of the country is in the stock market at all. And two, just about everything Trump has done—the tax cuts for billionaires, the trade and tariff wars that hurt rural communities and farmers, undermining health care enrollment and removing labor protections—all of these measures have taken dead aim at the people he claims to be fighting for.

All the time I hear good Democrats complaining, "But everyone knows the tax cuts were wrong and skewed to the wealthy!" A lot of voters do, yes, but many do not, and few understand the scale of the betrayal. Don't assume everyone reads the *New York Times* or Vox. If anything, assume that they don't, by far the safer bet.

Shame on us if we can't convince enough voters that they are cutting their own throats if they give Trump four more years to further feather the nests of the billionaires and large corporations. It's not that difficult: "Trump pushed through the biggest tax cuts for billionaires and corporations in history. He's cut funding for health care and education and job training. Rolled back regulations on the big banks that caused the recession and is doing the bidding of the sleazy payday loan and for-profit college rackets. The Democrat will raise taxes on the wealthy, cut your taxes, and invest in proven ideas in education and job training that creates good jobs."

One final important point, one that may seem to be gaining traction: the idea that at this moment in history, with populism on the march in countries all over the world, it's not about the economy. In 2020, it's about identity, culture, political correctness, provincial versus cosmopolitan, open versus closed, white nationalism, and so on and so on and so on. This theory proposes that what's going on now is simply that the partially buried id of the Republican Party—McCarthy, Goldwater, Nixon, Agnew, Palin, many others—has broken through to the surface big-time.

My answer: No doubt there is some truth there but only if you're talking about the base within the base, voters who do hear a different, scarier drummer with a beat that drives "Lock her up!" and "Send them back!" while their hero stands there, chin lifted to accept the reflexive idolatry, soaking it all in.

The subjects for us here and now are the undecided and persuadable and might-vote citizens—the ones who are motivated by wages, not the wackiness; by health care, not hate. They exist and they're more numerous than some of us might believe. These are the voters who will determine the outcome. This election is much more than just a battle of the bases, as critical as that will be.

We can't just throw up our hands and say racism, anti-immigrant sentiment, and misogyny are forces that are too powerful. That's Teflon for Trump for too many voters. There's no doubt it is a protective shield for him with his core base, but let's not paint with too broad a brush.

Playing offense, we can win because we have the goods. We just need to be smart, deploy them with discipline, and work hard. (I'll get into point-by-point details about how we can do this in the next chapter.) Playing defense against all the deception and lies perpetrated by the other side is trickier. Times have changed. Our campaigns have always been nasty affairs, our politics never for the faint of heart, but in the old days the main weaponry included whispered rumors and broadsheets and a few books passed around hand to hand. Then came radio and TV. Then came unrestricted chemical and biological warfare, in effect, insidious molecular attacks, minute by minute, second by second, on our computers, tablets, phones.

It's fair to say that 2016 presented us with a radical

escalation in this arms race. We'd never had a major party nominee whose first instinct was to lie about himself, then to attack (and lie about) his opponents, and then to prime the pump of the right-wing echo chamber to further the first two lying instincts. The unfairness and hypocrisy are mind-boggling. Just imagine that Barack Obama had violated campaign laws and matrimonial vows by illegally paying off his porn-star mistress with six-figure hush money in the days before the 2012 election. If reelected nevertheless, I guarantee you he would have been impeached by the Republican-controlled House on the morning of the first day of the next session, because that's how they roll. No question at all, and not much question that just about every Republican would have supported the cause in the Senate, while falling short of the two thirds required for conviction.

Now, four years later, we encounter yet another escalation. You were hoping that the nation's president would run a more elevated race than he did as a candidate? Dream on. Didn't you check your Twitter feed an hour ago and watch the news last night?! We Americans have elected some losers as president, but no sitting president has ever adopted such deceitful tactics as his default, go-to mode. In addition, this president has had at his beck and call the most powerful faux news/entertainment media empire in history, and it's growing larger all the time. Foreign leaders and governments launch missiles armed not with nuclear warheads but with misinformation designed to weaken American democracy. It is in their interest to have a buffoon leading America.

The bombardment has been effective. We have finally reached that nirvana of grifters and frauds worldwide: an almost fact-free environment, or as Kellyanne Conway prefers, "alternative facts." It should be no surprise that we are increasingly sorting ourselves into like-minded tribes speaking separate languages within echo chambers.

Lord knows it's tempting for #NeverTrumpers to do nothing but attack the man and his manner, which seem to have no bottom, but I'm not sure anyone can or should try to play his game. Trump is an idiot, but he has mastered politics as World Wrestling Federation art. Our nominee will have an overwhelming advantage in positive values—inspiration, ideas, facts and plans, and character—and they will be critical for energizing tough-to-register-and-turn-out citizens and even persuading the elusive swing voters. But we do have to be smarter on defense.

How? Let me begin the discussion with a stroll down memory lane, of better times—you know, way back, 2008 or 2007, when the preferred means of spreading lies in campaigns was the email chain. How quaint that must sound today, and at first those in the Obama campaign

HQ in Chicago didn't pay too much attention to them. The first ones sounded ludicrous. Educated in a madrassa in Indonesia; Muslim, not Christian; real father was not a Kenyan with a master's in economics from Harvard but a homegrown American radical; he'll impose Sharia law; he refuses to recite the Pledge of Allegiance; there's a grainy tape somewhere with Michelle Obama talking about "whitey." The list goes on and on—and all of it before Donald Trump's birther crusade. Those of us in the campaign knew all about the infamous Swift Boat Veterans for Truth in John Kerry's ill-fated run against George W. Bush just four years earlier, but those were heavily funded TV ads—legacy campaigning, out there for everyone to see and judge. But this stealth stuff on the internet? Who could take it seriously?

People on the internet, that's who. Our field organizers on the ground in the states started fielding questions about these crazy stories from our own supporters who were being recruited as volunteers. They said that they, of course, knew it was all nonsense, but they feared it would hurt us in the primary and even convince potential supporters that Obama would not be electable in the general election. Our press staffers were asked by reporters to comment. Eventually the candidate himself would get asked about some of these lies and smears when out on the trail. He and the rest of us tried our best to either ignore, laugh off, or fight these haphazardly through the primary.

Our defense left a lot to be desired. We should have taken this poisonous nonsense more seriously and armed our volunteers more effectively. We survived anyway, but once it was clear that Obama was going to be the nominee, we realized that the threat was real and could endanger the entire enterprise in November.

In June 2008, gearing up to face off against John McCain, we launched the website Fight the Smears. Doing this infuriated us, of course—the investment of time and money and having to acknowledge the sludge could hurt us. It was viewed as a big risk—or just plain stupid—by many in the political chattering class. They were still stuck in the era when the mantra was "Don't worry about it unless it shows up on the front page of the *New York Times* or on the evening news." Everything else, either ignore or deflect without elevating it. Acknowledging and itemizing the nonsense would only help spread it among computers throughout the country. Whatever you do, don't legitimize the purveyors of fraud by treating them the same way you would an attack on your tax or health care plans!

Good points, and we certainly had a vigorous internal debate about them. Conclusion: the quaint standards from the era of the legacy media are gone, along with the gatekeepers of ethical, fact-checked media. The new standard—not that there even is one—is much more difficult to police. What matters in the twenty-first century is that any one piece of content or rumor that is shared by even a few people can end up infecting millions of voters' devices in an instant, a political virus that no security software can catch or stop. The multiplier effect can be exponential. There is an old quip attributed to Winston Churchill and Mark Twain, among others, that a lie is halfway 'round the world before the truth can put its boots on. We can only wish this were still the case.

If the Obama effort had been a hierarchical campaign, not one fueled by millions of passionate supporters who were living part of their lives every day through and on behalf of Barack Obama, we might have decided against direct action. But we thought we had our own decentralized rapid-response army in the making, many of whom had digital savvy, so why not try to arm them with everything they needed to fight back against the sleaze machine and set them loose?

On the new website we listed every attack and smear, and then provided rebuttal information: news articles, fact-checking pieces, statements from Republicans condemning these smears, videos, our own talking points, and whatever else we had. Our troops could grab an appropriate link and attach it in a reply to a smear-laden email, share it with a questioning voter, and print out fliers if that's what it took.

I don't know how important that effort was ultimately to our victory in November, which ended up being by a much larger margin than we had thought possible in June, when we were given no better than an even-money chance to win. But I do know that if it had been just our campaign apparatus trying to fight back, it would have been an epically large game of Whack-a-mole, impossible to win. The website gave our millions of volunteers and supporters confidence to jump into the digital muck with their hazmat gear and suffocate the slimy lies bubbling up from the ooze.

I'm sure there were some voters on the fence who, sadly enough, needed to be reassured that Barack Obama was not a sleeper agent sent by Al Qaeda to do the terrorists' bidding from their new command post in the White House; and it certainly reassured the candidate and his family we were not going to take these lies and smears lying down.

And that was before Facebook and Twitter had made any serious penetration into the electorate. Just eight years later, look what they did to Hillary Clinton online: Pizzagate, child-sex rings, fatal health problems. Just about anything you could make up was said by someone, somewhere about her, and then sent out into world.

In 2020, the contours of what we will be dealing with are already clear. Whether the nominee is Pete Buttigieg, Elizabeth Warren, Joe Biden, Bernie Sanders, or one of the other contenders, Donald Trump, the Russians, Fox News, Rush Limbaugh, and the whole crazy but deadly network of smear peddlers and hate-mongers on the airwaves and the internet will claim that if the Democrat is elected, our borders will be opened to all comers, murder and rape will be daily horrors visited on our neighborhoods, our vets will be forgotten, criminals will be furloughed or paroled, the most ethical and honest administration in the history of the planet will be turned back into the swamp from whence it came, your taxes will go up 100 percent, you'll have to wait six months to see a doctor and grandma will have to wait six months for the death panel to convene, the economy will tank, and we'll have a new depression, which would be great for them because what they really want is a socialist America.

Oh, and for good measure, the Democrats support infanticide.

There will be nothing fancy about these pitches, no secret spin, no knucklers, curveballs, sinkers, brushback offerings. Just four-seam fastballs aimed directly at the candidate's head—and their aim is good. But wait a minute! What? Infanticide? Really? Will anyone other than wing nuts be tipped to believe the Democrats want to kill newborns? Anyone who truly is undecided on this race? Yes, there may be some voters who are very lukewarm on Trump, but the infanticide charge they read about in some dark corner of the internet, or maybe not so dark—think *Fox & Friends*—convinces them the Democratic nominee is too far gone to even consider, around the bend, gone off the deep end.

This kind of crap may also be the fuel to get more conservatives to donate money, give time, and get more involved in the Trump effort. Stopping infanticide can be quite the motivational rallying cry for those who believe that nonsense charge. It's a mistake for any of us to assume that a crazy lie bouncing around Facebook will not be believed. Everyday experience amply demonstrates that someone, somewhere, can believe just about anything. A content factory in Moscow can create an "article" stating that our Democratic nominee has been tied to an ongoing investigation into a pedophilia ring operating out of a pizza joint in Washington. And in twenty-four hours more people could see that smear then watch any of the major cable news shows that night.

It's tragic. Our presidential campaigns should not have to be fought this way; the stakes are too high and the issues too serious. But the truth is that we can't fight only the war we want to fight. We also have to play defense in the war that will be fought on Trump's behalf, and we have to win it. And when I say "we," I don't mean the Democratic National Committee. Or the nominee's campaign infrastructure. Or outside progressive groups. Or the media. Lord knows we need all those entities to get smarter and more effective at handling the *Mad Max: Fury Road* approach of the Trump campaign and the constellation of weaponry surrounding his approach. But the "we" I mean is us. As in you. As in me. We will become a decentralized, organic rapid-response machine, complementing smart efforts at the top, I hope, but definitely not waiting for them. We have to don those hazmat suits and do everything possible to keep people from drowning in the muck.

Much of this work will be frustrating, depressing, infuriating, tiring, and headache inducing, but I actually think it can also be fun. I believe there's a general sense, sadly, that progressives are weak or easily bullied, so when we fight back with gusto and confidence, the smear machine will be surprised and infuriated. I have no doubt that your down-to-earth conversation with a conflicted voter about how our nominee will cut her taxes and actually make our southern border safer with smart policies will outweigh the Siberian bot claiming the opposite. Surround your people with the truth.

CREATE

★ ★ ★

For most of the primary season leading up to the first voting in 2008, Barack Obama trailed Hillary Clinton by large margins in New Hampshire. We began closing the gap in December, and then on January 3 we convincingly won the Iowa caucuses, which was considered a pure three-way toss-up (remember John Edwards, anyone?). The momentum slingshot did the rest.

We had the big mo, big-time. Our final internal poll prior to the voting on January 8 had us winning New Hampshire by 8 points. The average of the public polls showed an even bigger lead. Everything was pointing up and to the right for the Obama team. The Granite State would wrap up the primary campaign, and Obama would be anointed the nominee by a landslide.

The punditocracy asked, "How large would Obama's win be? Will it be more than 10 points? More than 15 points? Will Clinton drop out if she loses that badly?"

Frankly, these were our only questions too. On Election Day, when the first exit polls showed us up by 5 points, our reaction was "Well, those numbers are clearly screwy; the final margin will be much bigger."

Actually, no. We lost by 3½ points.

Gut punch. Given the prior expectations, the loss in New Hampshire could have been a serious wound to Barack Obama's candidacy, potentially fatal. I could spend the rest of my life recounting what we—and I—did wrong leading up to the primary and probably not capture the extent of it all. And give Hillary Clinton and her campaign credit—they did a bunch of things right.

In any event, we were caught completely unprepared to lose in New Hampshire. The victory speech we were certain our candidate would give was pitch perfect, but we hadn't given a thought to a concession speech. It was our bad, and in the vacuum that swallowed us whole, Obama decided to give the victory speech, just adding a line of congratulations to Hillary Clinton. Was this an inspiring choice, or was he simply stunned by the loss and no one had any better ideas? Probably some of both.

The speech was based on the refrain "Yes We Can!," a translation of the call to arms employed by Cesar Chavez and the farmworkers movement during their long struggle for fair pay and better conditions. Obama had used that tagline in his 2004 Senate race in Illinois, and in 2008 we wanted it to play a more prominent role in the presidential race going forward. Such a rallying cry would suggest that history and conventional wisdom were wrong, that the cynics were wrong, that a candidate like Barack Obama could prevail and the country could truly change—but only if millions of Americans made the campaign their cause. Only if it was all about "We."

The concession speech gambit was viewed by most of the pros as quite unusual, by some as worse than that: tone-deaf and arrogant, failing to fully capture the magnitude of the defeat and what it meant to our chances. All wrong. Our supporters loved that speech because it underscored their understanding that this would be a long uphill battle, that there would be setbacks, but our candidate and campaign were convinced there was a path forward that relied on our citizen volunteers to make it happen. The day after the devastating loss in New Hampshire was our best online fund-raising day in the campaign up to that point, bigger than the day after the victory in Iowa the preceding week. It was our biggest day for signing up new volunteers, online and off.

Barack Obama had showed on the night before that even in the face of a stunning defeat he wasn't going to back down, and the following day his supporters showed they wouldn't either; they would have his back even when things hit a rough patch. Maybe it was the most successful "concession" speech ever.

You see where that twelve-year-old election story takes us in our 2020 discussion? This election will also be all about us—not them, not even him or her. The air campaign, the ground campaign; playing offense, playing defense; strategy, tactics—no matter what angle from which we look at this election, it's going to come down to us, you and me.

With all the sophistication possessed by the campaigns, and Russia, you may ask how a lone individual can compete on the message and persuasion battlefields. Wouldn't this amount to David versus Goliath, horse-drawn carriages versus shiny new cars, dial-up versus 5G?

I understand that you can't afford to waste time and energy tilting at windmills. Rest assured that you will not be wasting your time. Your engagement with persuadable voters can be incredibly effective and, if joined by enough others, can carry the day. When "me" becomes "we," suddenly there are millions of us out there fully engaged in this person-to-person effort, making a real difference "at scale," as we say in the Bay Area. It's the multiplier effect, where the virtuous circle can take us once it starts spinning.

As John Lennon once proclaimed, "One and one and one is three. . . ." Keep adding zeros . . . 300 . . . 3,000 . . . 3,000,000 . . . maybe more. Very possible. In both Obama campaigns, we eventually had millions of volunteers.

I'm certainly not suggesting that the Democratic nominee lay down the latest weapons of political warfare. The campaign, the party, the big outside groups will all be doing their thing, deploying data and analytics, testing a zillion ads on Facebook and other social media and internet sites to try to coax out that all-important click that will suggest where a voter is leaning, and why. Of course the Trump campaign, the Russians, and other unsavory actors will be doing likewise—maybe even more so.

But it's mandatory that the big institutional weaponry be coupled with a persuasion army working the ground, block by block, house by house, making the difference in moving enough truly torn and swing voters over to our nominee's column in a close election.

The candidate's official campaign and outside actors will have built a profile of millions of potential voters— the same cohort of voters that I hope you will be talking with. These profiles are based on census data, news and internet behavior, consumer data, voting history, and a whole bunch of other information put into the blender to pour out a likelihood-to-support score for each voter and some sense of the most effective messages and mediums to reach him or her. Kind of scary, I know, but that's where we are today, and it's only going to become more complicated. But these are demographic models, not real people.

Real people are better. You can ask them what will decide their vote, what problems and issues they're struggling with, what concerns they have with both Trump and the Democratic nominee. The best rule of thumb: don't even think about waiting for the party to do it. At this granular, one-on-one level, campaign talking points won't get the job done. I'm all for a well-executed and targeted ad from the Democratic National Committee, but I understand that it might not have a chance with the intended recipient. No matter how clever or compelling, it is still a passive experience. Do it yourself. Please. I firmly believe that nothing is as effective as two human beings having an honest, open, and real conversation. Your one-on-one "research" may square with what the data suggests. It may differ. Regardless, it will surely have more context, more specificity, and will provide a better understanding of how this individual can be reached and persuaded.

Most voters will likely never meet the nominee, so they will need reassurance from someone they know and trust—a neighbor, a family member, a colleague at work, a former schoolmate. You can and will refer to the campaign material as a helpful guide on the ins and outs of policy and issue differences, but if you want voters to open their ears instead of closing them, you want to sound like the neighbor you are, not a smooth-talking head on CNN.

You and you and you, in short. The sixty-year-old accountant in Pittsburgh who has never gotten involved in politics before this election? Perfect. The eighteen-year-old skateboarding whiz spending late afternoons on the streets, not on Xbox playing *Fortnite*? Sure! The life-long Republican, and known as such, now spending weekends at our nominee's local campaign office? Who could be better?

I realize that many people who follow politics, even intensely, and care deeply about issues hesitate to get down in the trenches because they've never done it, don't fully understand how, or are perhaps worried about the reaction from certain friends and family members. Maybe that's you. If so, you are one of those we've been waiting for, to quote our forty-fourth president.

Your impact would be far stronger than mine if we

were to have the same conversations and make the same points with the same people. An important aspect of your official work as a volunteer—maybe on a formal basis, perhaps as a precinct leader, whatever—is to find ways to demystify the process and the work for others who may be thinking about their own volunteering but have reservations or are nervous about diving into something so new and different.

I remember the first doors I knocked on in 1988. I had no idea what I was doing and thought the people who answered them would sniff that out in an instant. But the vast majority of conversations were pleasant, engaging, and interesting ("Why are you out here in the heat? Are you getting paid to do this? Why can't the Democrats get their act together and win the White House back?"). You just have to get out there, like most things in life, and you'll be just fine.

Bobby Kennedy, the best presidential campaign manager of all time, in my view, famously said in a speech in South Africa: "It is from numberless diverse acts of courage and belief that human history is shaped. Each time a man stands up for an ideal, or acts to improve the lot of others, or strikes out against injustice, he sends forth a tiny ripple of hope, and crossing each other from a million different centers of energy and daring, those ripples build a current which can sweep down the mightiest walls of oppression and resistance."

I draw no direct analogies between apartheid South Africa and America today, although I sometimes fear they may become warranted, especially if we don't win this election. Nor would I claim that all political campaigns qualify for the ripple-of-hope treatment. But this one certainly does. Sweeping away oppression and striking out against injustice? If that's not what we are doing here, well, what *are* we doing? As Obama often said in 2008, one voice can change a room, but that voice being joined by enough others can change our nation and the world. Strength is in numbers.

Defeating Trump by electing the Democrat is a mighty cause. That's all there is to it. I don't retract my early contention that November 3, 2020, will be a pivotal day in the history of our country.

The 2020 election is right in front of us. Your mission is not to turn every person into a lifelong voter, as much as we hope that will be the case. It is not to encourage everyone to become active in politics. It's not even to get them to look ahead and vote for Democratic candidates in the 2022 midterms. It's to get them to cast one vote in one election to get rid of one really horrible and dangerous president. That's it. Keep it in mind. If you are responsible for persuading just a handful of your fellow citizens who are on the proverbial fence—about voting at all or about voting for the Democrat—to register and then vote for our candidate, if you are joined by thousands and hopefully millions around the country, we will win.

Yes we can and yes we did in 2008 and 2012—and yes we will again in 2020.

We need a decentralized, fifty-state, rapid-response persuasion army. We also need a parallel content-creation army. There are a million ways to use your passion and creativity to advance the cause of defeating Donald Trump. If you have an idea you really like that can be put to video, song, paper, the sidewalk, or a sign, full speed ahead. Your overall goal is first to recognize your own skills, talent, and expertise that can be rallied to the cause, and second, to inspire other people to find and recognize the ways in which they can contribute. Numerous case histories follow.

Potential voters and volunteers might—no, *will*—respond better to these down-home creations than to official campaign jargon; they may be more inspired or, frankly, better identify with your content than they will with efforts from the campaign. You're quirky, even amateurish creation will be more effective than any ad created at a Belarusian content farm—or at DNC headquarters or in Trump Tower.

Your pitch may not be as polished or as professional, but that's exactly the point.

You can reach someone in your community or family with more authenticity and more understanding. Your effort will not be a poor substitute for what the official campaign or progressive groups could have done, would have done, might still do. Just the opposite! Your contribution will be, by definition, more authentic, more organic, more relatable—simply *better* in all important respects than what would come out through official channels.

Pertinent proof comes to us from that 2008 Obama campaign in the form of a video mash-up from the New Hampshire speech, created by will.i.am, formerly with the Black Eyed Peas, now of *American Idol* fame. Other notable musicians and performers, including Common, John Legend, and Scarlett Johansson sang or delivered some of the lines.

We had absolutely no input on that video. We didn't even know it was coming when it landed out of the blue on February 2, just days before the crucial set of twenty primaries and caucuses on a Super Tuesday that would be either our Waterloo or our stepping stone to the nomination and presidency. In those ancient days, Facebook and the other social media networks didn't have much reach. The will.i.am mash-up was one of the first clips to go viral, thanks mainly to young people, garnering more than twenty-five million views and tremendous attention from the press and on YouTube. The phenomenon drove many new donors and volunteers to join our campaign during this crucial window of opportunity, or disappointment, which was still possible.

What if the official campaign had produced exactly the same content, with the same talent? The impact would have been far more muted. Even to the supporters of a campaign, the officially produced campaign content has the veneer of propaganda. Now, I realize will.i.am is a celebrity, a subject for future discussion, but his video was so powerful because it was produced and disseminated organically. It demonstrated the true passion these artists had for Obama, which made it much more interesting, consumable, and shareable with Obama's confirmed supporters, and it led to new supporters and activism. Even back in campaign HQ in Chicago, when it started popping up on staffers' laptops, a new energy bounced around the office.

Remember the famous Obama Hope poster created by Shepard Fairey, the immensely talented graphic artist, visual designer, and activist? As with will.i.am's mash-up, Fairey's terrific piece was not a creation of the campaign or even anything we discussed with him. He created it and started disseminating it in early 2008, and within weeks it had begun to show up everywhere—on telephone poles, in dorm rooms, and in union halls. No, people don't vote because of signs, but we heard over and over again how much they loved the piece, and it further motivated them to lay it all on the line to elect Barack Obama. Whether it's a poster, a T-shirt, a hat, a bumper sticker, if you have talent in these spaces, put it to work on behalf of our Democratic nominee.

We, Democrats and progressives, have nothing like Fox and the conservatives' industrial-media-infotainment complex. The reasons are complex and beyond my scope here, but all that doesn't matter right now. What matters is offsetting that advantage with another of our own. It is absolutely mandatory that we weaponize our own social media and email lists. So, yes, that means you need to make sure you are signed up and active on Facebook, Instagram, Twitter, and Snapchat. For those of you who are adamantly anti-social media, I understand your feeling; the whole thing can be overwhelming, often toxic, but understand that your reticence plays right into the Trump playbook.

To be in the game you have to be in the arena, and social media is the primary arena this race will be fought in. Fact of life. If each of us spends just a couple of minutes a day moving message and content through our channels, thinking about smart ways to work with the local media, and doing some offline distribution, we can aggregate something that is real, authentic, and powerful.

There is not just strength but also comfort in numbers. When people see a video or any content from someone they construe as very much like themselves, making the same arguments they themselves have been wrestling with, they can be tipped to take action and vote. In 2008, many voters said on their own, unprompted, "I really can't believe I'm doing this, but I'm voting for Obama. We need a change and he'll be better for working people like me than McCain, who will just keep doing the same old things Bush did that got us into this mess." We invited some of these voters to be in ads. This worked. When people see someone making the leap, it creates a "permission structure" for following suit. Fancy term. Sounds suspicious, I know, but I've become a believer in it. It's getting people to do the thing they think they might do, even the thing they ought to do, by creating acceptable models so they'll feel better about doing it.

Facebook, the new public square, turbocharges the delivery of permission-structure content. At the same time, I'm all too aware that in terms of disinformation, doctored videos, audio bytes, and downright confusion, the platform presents a serious ongoing challenge to our nominee and our democracy.

That goes for its sister platform, Instagram, as well as Twitter and YouTube. However, there are some positive features about these platforms as they relate to politics: you can use them to create voter registration drives, remind people about early voting and absentee ballot deadlines on Snapchat and Twitter, and recruit for local Facebook groups that allow supporters of candidates to communicate and recruit others to join in the cause.

Many young people are opting not to sign up for Facebook accounts, preferring other social media platforms such as Snapchat and TikTok. Because that is where so much of the action is, and the voices of passionate young people are so powerful, if you fall into this cohort, you need to get on the platform. You can delete your account on November 4 if you must.

Trump ran a Facebook first campaign in 2016. He will do even more this time. As I write this sentence in August 2019, the Trump campaign is spending up the wazoo on Facebook advertising to reach voters in battleground states.

The big social media sites were weaponized by the Russians and others in 2016, but you can turn these networks into your own personal communications weaponry in 2020. The first step is to take an inventory and make sure you're in touch with everyone in your life who you think you should be in communication with, so you can stay in touch and you can also see what they're sending around. Write a list, type into your notes on your phone, think comprehensively.

Make sure your own personal network does not restrict membership to only the politically like-minded. Now is not the time to prune your uncle John, who is MAGA through and through. His presence allows you to see firsthand and in real time what propaganda he is seeing and spewing on behalf of Trump. Do you have a decidedly nonpolitical but certain-to-vote friend from work? Send a friend request with the intention of expressing sympathy for a true undecided voter trying to negotiate this hellscape of misinformation. Help this friend sort fact from fiction.

The social media landscape can be a modernized version of the Fight the Smears website in 2008, a one-stop shopping destination of refutation, so millions of supporters around the country and on the internet can fight back with links, videos, and credible independent voices.

See a Facebook post from your third cousin saying the Democratic nominee hasn't paid his or her taxes in twenty-five years? Don't simply get into a frustrating and unsatisfactory exchange voicing your opinion. Respond with something like, "Jennifer, I'm sorry, but that's just not true. The Democratic nominee has paid an effective tax rate of 28 percent over the last ten years. We know this because he/she has released his/her tax returns. Has Donald Trump? We'll never know but speculation is that he paid zero or close to it in taxes, despite being the self-proclaimed billionaire, while all the rest of us pay our fair share."

Then link to a Fox dispatch or a *Wall Street Journal* article that covers the topic and makes the points above. Again, the nominee's campaign should make this research easy for us, but if not, or if you think you can find something better, and quite possibly you can, a few keystrokes will find you what you need.

Did I say link to Fox and the *Wall Street Journal*? Absolutely. It's more effective to post genuine information from what will be seen as credible sources to those voters we have the best chance of reaching. Maybe your cousin Jennifer has zero chance of changing her mind or her vote (especially if you send her an article from *The Nation* or by Paul Krugman in the *New York Times*, or a clip from Rachel Maddow), but maybe one or two people in your network will see the exchange and factor it into their decision.

This principle always applies: look online for compelling,

shareable content that makes the best case against Trump and for the Democratic candidates' leadership and ideas. Then put these arguments in your own words. You have an authentic message to communicate. Don't be concerned that you may differ from the official talking points, or you are sharing unpolished content. The more real your engagement is, the more it sounds like you, not me, and the more effective it will be. Tell a story, show a picture—that's what will move people, not vague threats or promises about gross national product or ozone depletion.

In the introduction I noted this election's "90 percent problem": most of us live in a state that isn't a battleground. But this is where social media becomes very useful: online we are all one big country. Online there are no state lines. Maybe a response you post will have no effect with most people who see it because they already agree (or emphatically disagree) with you. That's okay. Most of us have connections throughout the country, so a few people in your feed may live in Wisconsin or Florida or another battleground state or have a cousin or college roommate there. They had seen in their feeds some of the same bullshit you responded to in your post, but they'd had no idea how to fight back. Now they have such an idea, and they can then pass along the message in their more embattled communities.

It's a long and winding road online. Rest assured, that powerful post will somehow end up in the feeds of people in the battleground states, where they grab that same content and insert it into some of the discussion happening in their own online battleground communities. Welcome to the rapid-response army. From your haven in San Diego or Birmingham, you're having an impact in all theaters of this war. And for everyone who sees your response in your feed or email chain, hopefully you have shown them the way, and encouraged more people to do just as you did: get into the fight. And the virtuous circle strengthens as their responses reach and encourage others.

And then there is the advanced social media campaigning, understanding the clever use of hashtags, native content, photos, what gets pulled. Many of you, certainly the digital or almost digital natives, know more about this than I do. For those who don't, go get an education! I know I need to. These simple techniques can rocket your posts way beyond your own personal universe.

Intensely personal expressions of the stakes in this election can be extraordinarily compelling. An eighteen-year-old in Ocala, Florida, who will be voting in her first election, creates a series of iPhone videos for YouTube capturing the stakes this year. One video might be about the impending doom from climate change, especially pronounced in Florida. A disproportionate percentage of Trump's supporters will not have to bear the weight of their collective failure on this threat, which is exacerbated by their ignorance and selfishness, but Gen Z will actually be alive and living through the worst of the predictions if the curve is not bent drastically enough on emissions.

The video captures the urgency of the moment—the cataclysmic fallout of famine, floods, unlivable heat, and historic migration. Gen Z wants a chance to thrive, not merely to cope with this apocalypse. Perhaps this young voter says the Democratic nominee is not perfect, but where the future of the planet is at stake, the nominee will get us back into the Paris climate accords, reverse all of Trump's reversals of President Obama's environmental executive orders, and try to enact a version of the Green New Deal or key parts of it.

Our nominee, no matter how skilled and persuasive, could give fifty speeches on the urgency of the climate threat and the plans to tackle it, but their collective impact on eighteen-year-old voters throughout the country will be insignificant compared with the power released by this video from the young voter in Ocala. It will be more interesting. More accessible. More relatable. More believable. More actionable. Young voters can identify with it.

Maybe it gets them to decide to do more personally, to volunteer in addition to voting. And they will likely share it, perhaps with comments, or send a like. More ripples will spread throughout that cohort and the country.

Or our young voter in Ocala may post another video on student loans because she's already scared to death about what will happen as she begins her own debt-laden college experience, having seen older siblings coming out of college with crushing debt. Trump is in the tank with the lenders and the for-profit university sharks. The Democrat wants to make community college free for all and likely will have a plan for all other colleges—perhaps middle-class students or below will have free college tuition, maybe with some interesting service and income-based repayment models.

A second-term Trump will just double down on approaches and policies that screw young people. With Democrats in office again, young people have some reason to hope things will change with our nominee. That message will be far more compelling coming from a peer. It will be authentic and present the point with words that are inherently nonpolitical.

This same really busy eighteen-year-old will capture the experience of volunteering in a YouTube video as she heads out on a canvassing shift with some friends on a

Sunday afternoon, showing what it feels like to inform voters in the community that their future depends on this election, and to persuade other young voters not to sit it out or vote third party.

Be sure to record the hilarious moment when an ignorant Trump supporter slows down his car as he passes by your group on the street and yells out, "Finding illegal votes for your candidate, I see!" If you and your team do much canvassing on the streets, you will encounter such negative "feedback," I guarantee—and more than once. No problem. Take it as proof that you're making an impression, because you are. Team MAGA is scared because you're out there.

Let's say ten thousand young people throughout the country each make their own videos capturing their volunteer experience and imploring others to join the cause. Maybe another five young people who see each video decide to get more involved. Amazingly, ten thousand volunteers turn into fifty thousand just through a few minutes of video on your phone and a quick upload. Fifty thousand is a powerful number in any community, but especially in battleground precincts.

The kids are more than all right. Their power of devoting themselves to a cause is so infectious that swing voters will be interested in why an eighteen-year-old is out knocking on doors instead of staring at a device in the bedroom, perhaps like their own kids are doing; other young people will be curious and, I hope, be motivated by their leadership and activism. The enthusiasm can have a powerful effect on other family members, all the way up to grandparents, who may be so inspired by the grandkids' commitment that they'll want to join them and give time themselves.

A Republican voter who voted for candidate Trump but cannot stomach President Trump and will vote Democratic has the foundation to create and share powerful and inspiring content. It may be as simple as turning on the phone and riffing:

"I voted for Trump last election. I saw it as the lesser of two evils, but I also thought that no matter what, Trump would stick up for the little guy, the working person in this country. Now I see that that was all an act. Everything he's done, like the huge tax cuts for the top 1 percent, has been for people like him. We have enough billionaires in this country, and they certainly don't need extra handouts and help from the government. We need workers to make more. That's why while I don't agree with everything they stand for; I'm voting for the Democrat, who, when push comes to shove, will make decisions with people like me in mind, not the Wall Street gazillionaires."

Post it, share it, create other videos like it. Odds are

you'll reach someone who is wrestling with some of these same questions, and your video may influence them to make their own video.

Does this extended scenario seem utopian? Maybe, but it matters. It's another virtuous circle, not from doing anything extraordinary but from capturing the feelings, views, and activity you are already experiencing and sharing them with your network—who may just share it with theirs. Plus it will just feel good to articulate how you are feeling about this election and what you are going to do about it.

Are you canvassing in the suburbs outside of Madison, Wisconsin, on a beautiful Saturday in early September? Combine social media expertise with real-world, boots-on-the-ground activism by capturing the experience through your own Instagram story: the excitement (or chaos) in the Dane County HQ as you get your instructions and information on the turf and the voters you will be trying to talk to today; the peace and beauty of the neighborhoods as you walk through them; your pride after persuading a voter on your list to support our nominee; the fun banter back and forth with your friend who's working the other side of the street; the mandatory local bratwurst and beer you share with other volunteers after your shift is done as you reminisce about the poignant and funny conversations you had with your voters and share that great feeling of pouring yourself into a mission you believe is as important as any you may see in your lifetime, and definitely as important as any you have seen to date.

Others in Wisconsin and throughout the country will see your Instagram story. They will share it with others, some of whom will decide to hit the doors the next Saturday afternoon. Some may decide to head to a local phone bank in California and New York, calling rather than canvassing into battleground states, making a big difference and also having a wonderful shared experience with their fellow phone bankers. Some may not physically be in a battleground state, but you know the mantra: online there are no state lines. Your video will be seen in all fifty states. Moreover, you may have a key congressional race in your district, and our next president will need as many allies as possible to move forward the progressive agenda this country so desperately needs. Your video may cause your neighbors to get out and help these great local candidates too.

Your four hours on the ground in Dane County, captured on social media, will have huge direct and indirect impacts. Directly you will be engaging with the most critical voters in the presidential contest, and hopefully you helped persuade a few to support our candidate or to vote if they were unsure of doing so. Joined by thousands of others throughout Wisconsin on that same Saturday afternoon, you collectively have taken big strides in returning the Badger State to its rightful electoral color. And it's OK that blue will conflict with Badger red just for a night.

You might also get more adventurous and orchestrate a bigger event. If you know the former sheriff and a local crime victim activist, and if they are willing to say they trust the Democratic nominee to keep us safe, you have all you need for an effective event. Send out a note to the local paper announcing an event at two p.m. tomorrow on the Manitowoc County Courthouse steps, when former Sheriff Young and crime victims' advocate Wright will respond to Donald Trump's outrageous assertion about all the rapists and murderers overrunning our society. People with experience can explain how our candidate will focus on resources in your own community for real threats, not scapegoating immigrants and scaring people, Trump's favorite ploy—his only ploy, really. They can show how our candidate will create better-paying jobs and invest in education, which will keep more people out of prison, and how the Democrats want to reform the criminal justice system—more rehabilitation, less recidivism.

Do not worry that these are not "professionally" planned events. They won't be perfect. The answers to questions by your star performers might be a bit off. Maybe it rains.

Whatever. What people in your town will see are people they know and trust taking issue with Trump, the fearmongering liar, and educating people a bit on the Democratic nominee's approach to the criminal justice system and related issues.

Now, about email. In the first Obama campaign, email lies and slander were the central battlefield. In a texting/ Snapchat world, emails as a political weapon—or quite frankly, email as a tool for anything—can seem prehistoric, relegated by social media to a more distant theater of war. Maybe they are archaic, but there will be millions of email chains bouncing around the country throughout the general election campaign, especially among, ahem, older voters. Said with all due respect! Post-fifty, I'm closing in on that label myself and still remember when I found email to be groundbreaking and revelatory.

But in a close race, you have to be prepared to compete everywhere. Email can still be a potent arena to spread misinformation at warp speed that gets shared and shared again, and pretty soon you are looking at big numbers. And older voters tend to, well, vote.

Fortunately, the tactics for dealing with weaponized— or just downright crazy—email chains are very similar to social media rapid response. Know or heard about someone who voted for Trump but rues that error of judgment and would never do it a second time? Capture him on video and distribute through your email channels. Someone who didn't vote in 2016, but now regrets that and can't take any more of this debased White House? Capture and share. A lifelong Republican who has never even imagined voting for a Democrat—until now. Beautiful raw material to be bouncing around the country's inboxes.

Finally, newspapers may be considered beyond prehistoric by many, but don't kid yourself—newspapers still reach millions of people, especially a lot of our older citizens who are by far the most likely to vote.

Write op-eds and letters to editors to point out the simple fact that Trump is the most fiscally reckless president in history. Ask how true conservatives could support the most humongous deficits in history—and not with programs that produce jobs but by the largest giveaway to the rich in history.

A quick word to campaigning celebrities. You're probably not one of them, but to Angelina, Brad, LeBron, George, Jennifer, and all you other A-listers who may be perusing this volume—if you do happen to be tuned in, I implore you to think more expansively about how you can use your creativity and prodigious social media assets to further the cause you support. Like it or not, you can create waves, not ripples, *waves*. Exhibit number one was that electrifying impact of will.i.am's mash-up of Obama's concession speech in New Hampshire in 2008, as reported above.

Now, you celebrities are no match or substitute for the combined might of the grassroots' social media activism and ground game drawn from the tens of millions of supporters of the Democratic nominee. We have just seen—and will see again—how that works. But we also need to exploit the fact that this nominee in 2020 will enjoy the support of most of you who have tens of millions of followers. Your passionate activism can be a major advantage for us. With all due respect to those who have toiled in the political vineyards for years and decades, a truly dedicated creative class will generate more effective and clever content and arguments than we professionals have been able to deliver on issues like climate, taxes, health care, Cuba, and many more.

Just imagine, if all the celebrities with social media assets of more than ten million followers would just once a week post a response to a common lie bouncing around the internet about the Democratic nominee, that wave would reach a far larger audience than Sean Hannity could ever hope to and thereby accelerate the building of the national rapid-response network I have described here. It would be a tragedy if this asset were not leveraged effectively and fully to win the most important election of our lifetime. Ideal would be a coordinated campaign among you. Any volunteers?

Or imagine you're an actor with a massive social media following who travels to a small town in Pennsylvania with no film crew, just the phone. Say Mount Pleasant, a town of four thousand less than an hour outside of Pittsburgh. You hit a local diner like the Main Street Deli and Café and engage the patrons in a discussion about the election, and shoot a little amateurish video while you're at it. You edit the piece in the car on the way to the airport and before you take off, you post it to your millions of followers and ask them to share it. By the time you're back on whichever coast you live on, you've achieved virality, reaching far more people than are watching the highest-rated Fox News show on any night. You are not spitting into the foul wind. You are standing up to it with powerful weaponry—your voice, your art, and your massive audience.

Imagine a singer (or maybe a band) who decides to record a musical call to action for the climate and the election, releases it on YouTube and other platforms, asks the fans to share it, implores them to vote, and provides how-to links for volunteering. That call to action would be more effective than three speeches in the candidate's "climate week." As someone who has put a lot of time into planning and thinking about such speeches, this is a sobering fact. But the world has changed. Trump knows this—it's a large reason why he won in 2016. The bottom line is that Trump has the Fox/Sinclair/talk-radio axis of evil echoing and amplifying his every argument and wild-ass assertion.

Or maybe a basketball star with tens of millions of followers, who each time they travel for a road game, records a quick video. In town to play Giannis and the Milwaukee Bucks, they say, "Hey Wisconsin. I hope we win tonight in Milwaukee, but the bigger contest is the presidential election. It could all come down to Wisconsin. So, I want you all to make sure you're registered to vote, you have a plan for voting, and you're giving whatever time you can to the campaign. Go to democraticnominee.com to find out how. We have to beat Trump. But it will take a team to do it." The more specific and actionable, the better. Less sentiment, more strategy.

You have been given more than the proverbial fifteen minutes of fame. How about using a mere fifteen minutes of your fame a week to defeat Donald Trump?

As discussed in the previous chapter, playing offense requires sharing our candidate's ideas and plans and attesting to his or her character. Playing defense requires calling out all the opposition's lies, deception, and attempts to sow division—exposing them for the utter bullshit they are. Let's talk about specific ways to deal with voters one-on-one, sometimes playing offense, sometimes defense.

Let's start with the deeply conflicted voter who testifies: "No way I can vote for Trump. But the Democrats have gone too far off the deep end. They support killing babies after they are born, want no immigration laws, and are gonna raise taxes on everyone. I'm going to vote for the third-party candidate to send a message to both parties."

Music to Trump Tower and Putin's dacha.

"I hate Trump, but they're all pretty much the same. A Democrat wins, and nothing will change. What's the point of voting?"

More music to pro-Trump ears. Both sentiments fulfill a fundamental aim of the Trump campaign: taint our party and nominee to such a degree that such voters either don't vote or choose a third party instead. Here's what we want instead from this conflicted cohort:

"I voted for Gary Johnson last time. I didn't like Trump or Clinton. Trump's been even worse as president than I thought. I liked Obama OK, but I'm not sure about this new Democrat—but the choice is better than

Trump, or at least less annoying and embarrassing. And the only way to get rid of Trump is to have the Democrat win. I don't want to throw my vote away this time."

Now that's the tune of a Democratic victory song. The question is how to guide voters away from those first two answers and toward the last answer. My recommendation when talking with them: do not launch into a speech about how horrible Trump is, or how great the Democrat is. I recommend something simple that acknowledges where the voter is right now:

"I completely get that. I struggle with it too. Let's pretend for a minute that who we elect as president could make a difference. What would be most important to you to see happen?"

If they share something—they want more done about the climate, or someone who cares about working people, or resolving the national crisis of student loans and debt, or ending corruption—you have your opening. If you happen to have knowledge about the issue—and the related case against Trump and for the Democratic nominee—jump in and make the case. You don't have the facts or the nominee's position on the issue? That's OK. Ask this voter for contact info and make sure you send good information.

Meet them where they are—but go no further. Spare

them the lecture on the responsibilities of citizenship and how awesome our nominee is. They're not in the mood for it. Such exhortations usually fall flat.

Flat, just like one of my favorite riffs to lay on young people at colleges and other venues:

"In our country we settle our disputes at the ballot box, not the battlefield. And even the one exception to that, the Civil War, was propelled by the result of the 1860 election. Every war we fight or don't. Tax we cut or raise. Health care we provide or deny. Air we clean or dirty. Roads we pave or not. On every single issue the results of those questions and decisions flow directly back to whom we elect. I get it that politics these days can seem small, silly, depressing, and hopeless. But it's the system we have, and the people we elect in this flawed system have the same power, and likely more, than Washington, Lincoln, and Roosevelt. Opting out is surrendering our future, your future, to the old cynical protectors of the status quo."

Maybe that works well with the kids; I'm not even sure, but I can't help myself. You can do better; when talking with voters on or anywhere near the fence, do not get up on your soapbox like that. They don't need speeches. They need real talk. With college students who are getting killed by student loans from a for-profit university and no one is helping, a productive response might be:

"I'm sorry. I know that's hard. The Democratic nominee may not have all the answers but will crack down on those for-profit colleges. Trump has made it easier for them to duck accountability and screw students. The Democrat has promised to increase the number of people eligible for Pell Grants. Trump has cut them. And the Democrat has interesting ideas about loan forgiveness and income-based repayment. Trump could not care less about your individual situation. He always puts the lenders before students. Do we really want four more years of this?"

Maybe that spiel won't get the job done. Most likely they won't tell you then and there. But you've planted a seed. Maybe you send them some reinforcing info. You connect them with a young person who shares their major concern and is voting for the Democrat. Turn a random conversation into a peer-to-peer conversion.

Many voices and many types of content will be essential for conveying the superiority of our candidate into the digital bloodstream. One would be a farmer from southwestern Wisconsin who whips out her phone in June and says while sitting on her tractor, "Trump's trade war is killing me. Most farmers agree. I also don't like the example he's setting for kids like mine. I gave Trump a chance last time, but I'm voting for the Democrat, who can't be any worse and is at least saying all the right things about ending Trump's dumb war on farmers. It won't take too many of us to flip Wisconsin. I might even paint a sign on my barn saying 'Dump Trump.'"

Once the sign is painted, she can post a photo on Instagram and also capture by post and video some of the good—and funny—reactions to it. This content is a trifecta of goodness: great message about the effect of Trump's trade war on a farmer in a key battleground state, a video that may encourage others who feel the same way to follow suit and create their own content, and a sign on a barn—instant attention-getter. There are unlimited similar options. Ask yourself these questions: What visible areas do you have on your property? What image can you create that drivers will see and snap and post? Live in Florida on a route busy with tour busses all the time? Hit 'em with a sign or poster.

Because we live in an increasingly visual world, you might create signs and posters for your yard or windows, and paint the side of the barn. Search for infographics and charts that are crystal clear at a glance.

A quick Google search will yield dozens, hundreds, thousands of sites demonstrating with graphs and pie charts that the lion's share of Trump's tax cuts went to the wealthy and large corporations. They show how almost all of the largest of the big corporations used their share of the boondoggle to buy back stock to feather the already gilded nests of the wealthy, not to create jobs as promised, further demonstrating how the reckless tax cuts have blown up the deficit.

Copy the results of your search onto fliers and drop them at doors throughout your community. Make the point that these horribly misguided policies were also a complete betrayal of Trump's claim that he would fight for the "forgotten" American. Instead, he forgot about most of America and did all he could for the top 1 percent.

Medicaid will be a pivotal issue throughout the country. If you live in a state like Virginia, which expanded Medicaid, and you or a family member receive treatment you didn't have before, share that story and testify that four more years of the incumbent puts your health at risk. Tell a story about someone with a disabled child or an aging parent whose doctor visits will be cut if Trump and the Republicans get four more years to gut the Affordable Care Act, aka Obamacare.

It could be that your child has respiratory troubles, and you were so hopeful when the Obama administration cracked down on mercury emissions from plants in your area—a commonsense initiative that Trump's stooges have now reversed, allowing more toxins to be released into your community's air. Your child's very health is at stake.

Maybe you work at a company in the green energy space that started and flourished due to support during the

Obama years. Tell voters that the Democrat will expand such initiatives. Trump and his political appointees in the pertinent federal agencies will do their best to crush them and kill jobs.

Playing offense with all possible voters and conflicted voters, we need to make sure there is plenty of content that they can see and share as they work through their decision. Maybe it's a pie chart. Maybe it's personal testimony. Maybe it's a big sign on the barn, or a sandwich board on your Labrador. Make it factual. Make it personal. Make it count. Keep it going until November 3.

On the big issues, we have both powerful truth and powerful truth tellers on our side. Regarding climate change, for example, every major environmental group, scientists, high-profile voices like Leonardo DiCaprio's that have credibility on climate, and credentialed politicians like Al Gore are likely to have statements, op-ed pieces, and interviews explaining how the Democratic nominee is all that stands between us and climate catastrophe. Share that content with a young, concerned voter who has "heard" otherwise.

Health care professionals, experts on public health, even Barack Obama himself will have produced scads of material on Medicaid and other health care issues, all driving home the point that it's Democrats and Democrats only who will build on Obamacare, not destroy it, and fight for more coverage for more people and further bring down costs.

As for immigration, elected officials, including sheriffs who patrol the southern desert border, Dreamers, business leaders, and many other supporters of sane immigration laws will have declared on the record that Trump is the most anti-immigrant president in U.S. history. His Democratic opponent will be proimmigrant and committed to fighting for comprehensive immigration reform that will finally solve our immigration challenges. Univision and Telemundo will also provide meaty content evaluating the two candidates on immigration policy, plans, and attitudes.

There is no shortage of good content, no shortage of ways to share it. Let there be no shortage of supporters doing this.

Trump unleashes lies at an unprecedented rate, and his accomplices in the Fox News/Sinclair/Breitbart media-entertainment vortex from hell defend every single one. It won't get better as we approach the election. The voter-suppression and voter-confusion efforts we saw in 2016 will be perpetrated on a much grander scale in 2020, some based in Moscow, Belarus (and other foreign locations), Washington, or Trump Tower. Young voters will be served ads claiming that the Democratic nominee is in bed with the fossil-fuel industry and won't do anything on climate change. Health care sensitive swing voters will hear that our candidate is opposed to universal health care. Young Latino voters will be told that Trump is the only candidate for comprehensive immigration reform, that the Democrat has no plan.

Unbelievable claims—except that they aren't unbelievable to everyone. In fact, the Trump campaign is already spending millions on these types of digital ads in core battleground states while our candidates battle it out in the primary. We have a lot of catching up to do.

As already explained, the Republicans' hope is that some anti-Trump voters will give up on the Democrats too, and be driven to third-party candidates or not vote at all. For us, stopping this drive to suppress turnout is, to borrow the term from NASA, "mission critical." We can't let these incredibly duplicitous tactics succeed.

We don't have to match the Trump machine blow for blow, but we do have to unleash responses in such numbers and in so many mediums that his one huge presidential megaphone is matched not with volume, because that's impossible, but with numbers. Millions of smaller megaphones.

In the opening chapter I talked about how important it is to fight back—play defense—and proposed some general ideas about how to do so. Now let's examine how to use our own specific voices proclaimed into our own, maybe homemade, megaphones.

You see something in your Facebook feed from one of your old college friends about a "study" demonstrating that if the Democrat is victorious, crime will rise 50 percent and rapes and murders by undocumented immigrants will triple. Take a minute to shake your head in frustration, sigh in sadness, but then respond calmly and by sharing content that shows the Democrat's commitment to increasing funds for local enforcement; stats showing that immigrants commit fewer violent crimes than those native born; our candidate's commitment to solving at long last the immigration challenge with comprehensive reform, including smart, humane, technology-based border security. It'll take you just a few seconds to search out the good stuff. Put up links to those interviews, statements, and videos in a comment on his post to give something new to think about to those who roll their eyes and say it's a choice of the lesser of two evils.

Maybe there is one person in this particular Facebook chain who will factor in the information you share. Two is better, but one is okay. Any "lesser of two evils" voters will understand the profound differences—and the profound stakes—for them and their communities in this election.

Even if zero people in this chain are directly influenced, others in the feed who share your views and are committed to defeating Trump will now have more confidence to engage in their own rapid response. They will have their own ideas about how to do so, weaponry from their own personal arsenal.

Now that crazy Uncle John is at it again, sending a new email full of misinformation, the infanticide conspiracy theory, for example, your wisest course of action is to take a moment to inwardly vent your frustration and sadness, then get down to business:

"Uncle John, I respect that you support Trump. As you know, I do not support Trump. While I don't support everything about the Democratic nominee, I think on balance our country would be better off with that nominee in the White House than four more years of Trump. But let's make it an honest debate. You have plenty of arguments to make on Trump's behalf that are true and maybe persuasive to some. The article/video/infographic you just shared to suggest the Democratic nominee supports infanticide is a lie. No credible person in our country, much less a presidential candidate, supports infanticide. My candidate is pro-choice, yes. Trump used to be pro-choice; now he says he is pro-life. So there's that difference. My candidate wants abortion to be safe, legal, and rare. Trump would like to see it outlawed—for every woman.

Check out this article below from the *Wall Street Journal*, hardly a liberal source, that captures the candidate positions on abortion and makes clear the infanticide charge is a hideous lie."

I realize that sending such a message will likely engender an intolerably large number of replies, perhaps from people from both sides. If you choose to weigh in again, perhaps simply respond with, "Here's another article from another conservative source."

Your search will yield plenty to choose from, pointing out the truth.

Again, maybe it will have an impact on someone on the chain. Maybe not. But it gives both confidence and ammunition to others on the chain and may even give pause to some Trump supporters about the content of their own chain or posts on infanticide. Maybe they will think they are not on supersolid ground.

I know some of you who may be younger or live on the coasts may think talk radio died in the 1980s, but it's alive and well in many parts of America, mostly in Trump and maybe-Trump country. And there are lots of sports call-in shows, where the presidential race is sometimes a hot topic along with why my Philadelphia 76ers may win the NBA Championship.

Tune in sometime and try to target a show originating in a maybe-Trump region. If the blowhard host or deranged caller makes a patently spurious charge about Democrats wanting to throw open the border, take health care away from veterans, free all prisoners regardless of how violent their offense was, et cetera, grab your phone and wait your turn, and then, before they know what's hit them, point out the indisputable fact that Trump is the most fiscally reckless president in history, the champion deficit increaser, and not due to programs that also produced jobs and infrastructure but with the largest giveaway to the rich in history.

Go right at them. If you get the opportunity, use the same points you would online, provide websites or sources people should look up online for verification.

You'll drive them nuts. The Hannitys, Carlsons, and Limbaughs of the world, as well as the second-string local talk show hosts, simply cannot handle being directly challenged. They bully, bloviate, and dominate.

Even if they taunt you, even if you convince no one, the Trumpsters will be forced to spend precious airtime defending their man, not launching errant missiles at our nominee. Time of possession is important in sports and politics. So is setting the tempo of the game.

Also, there will be people listening in who actually are going to vote for the Democratic nominee, even if in small numbers. Perhaps they get enjoyment out of all the crazy talk or want to know what the other side is peddling. I happen to believe that from time to time it's a very smart thing to drop into crazy town and listen to Limbaugh and the rest. I certainly find it motivational.

Besides, piercing the reality distortion field they live in can be a whole lot of fun.

Maybe you're listening to the *Buck Sexton Show* in the evening, running on WMEQ in Eau Claire, Wisconsin. The host is leading a discussion about whether Trump has delivered on his promise to drain the swamp. He believes Trump has succeeded—look how many scientists have left certain agencies!—and he welcomes callers with other examples of how swamp-drainy Trump has been.

You call in and say, "No doubt that is one of his appeals. But in fact, it's the biggest promise he's broken. He has used the presidency to personally enrich himself and his family, has likely illegally meddled into business mergers and acquisitions. No administration has had more lobbyists working in it or designing its policies. DC is now more corrupt and swampier than Wall Street and Hollywood, thanks to Donald Trump."

And have the objective content ready to cite, if you get the chance.

Say Trump spends a week in September barnstorming the handful of true battleground states on what might as well be labeled the Democrats Love Rapists and Murderers Tour. Much more likely to happen than not, sadly. Let's say you live in one of those battleground states, Wisconsin, say, in the town of Manitowoc. The Democrats' nominee will drive the party's different message that week, let's hope effectively. The nominee may have press events scheduled in Madison and Milwaukee to reference the absurdity of the attacks and fire back. Local Democratic officials, current and former law enforcement voices, and crime victims will be on hand. The campaign may run some ads pushing back. All good, but the circus that is Trump will surely gobble up lots of news and social media. Our events will get some statewide TV and radio coverage—not as much as Trump's stuff, but some—but what the campaign won't likely be able to execute is a local event in your hometown, Manitowoc.

It is therefore imperative that local Democratic supporters are readily available to all media and are armed with good talking points and easily shared content. You will serve as good rapid responders on the spot. Same principle here. Don't get spooked; don't be afraid you won't be "professional" enough; and don't worry that you don't have a suitable podium. Who cares that you've never done anything like this? The local voices, including yours, will be much more trusted by your neighbors than those from the "liberal" big counties. They won't drown out Trump, but they will ensure that the Manitowoc *Herald Times Reporter* and WMOT, the local radio station, give the Democratic nominee's positions prominence. Thanks to you.

REGISTER

★ ★ ★

Registration—can voter registration really bend the curve toward victory, or is it just nibbling around the edges? Let me tell you one quick story about the campaign volunteers in one state whose voter registration work altered the national campaign strategy. The state is Florida, where both early public polling and our own surveys months before Election Day suggested that the Sunshine State was out of reach for Barack Obama in 2008.

Wrong.

He won with 51 percent of the November tally. Nevertheless, four years later, in the run-up to the election, Florida was considered again out of reach by many, including some in our own campaign. In fact, it was looking worse than had been predicted in 2008. In mid-October, some news organizations even declared the state out of reach for the president; Romney would win. These organizations therefore declared they would stop wasting their money on polling.

At the campaign HQ in Chicago and the White House in Washington, we once again had to decide whether to tilt at windmills (if you listened to the political chatter). But we started focusing on a different interpretation. Florida had a really fluid population (and still does), with people moving in and out all the time, large numbers of young voters crossing the eighteen-year-old threshold every year, and a large number of unregistered minority voters who were now eligible to vote. All in all, there was a huge target population of potential supporters, invisible (and thus uncounted) to the pollsters. We thought that if we could dive into this "target pool" with enough "human capital"—volunteers—to get enough registered we could adjust the electorate in our favor—winning the game we wanted to play, not the other way around.

The brilliant number crunchers in Chicago and their very cool software modeled the likely Florida outcome after being given different registration numbers. Good news: if we could register more than 250,000 from the favorable Obama cohorts, we could win in a squeaker, and in our winner-take-all system, 49.9 percent is worth squat, but 50.1 percent is as good as a landslide.

We knew we had an incredibly large and passionate grassroots volunteer base in the Sunshine State, and they didn't balk at the numbers. They believed they could register that many people. They were adamant, and the candidate was tempted, but as an extremely logical guy, he wanted to make sure we were making a sound decision before we poured resources, energy, and his time into Florida. Now remember, he had led an extremely successful voter registration effort in Illinois in 1992 (the first Bill Clinton election) called Project Vote. He knew what was possible when a large number of unregistered or improperly registered voters are engaged by sufficient human and financial resources to get them properly on the voting rolls. Magic, that's what.

Most candidates would have written off Florida as a lost cause in 2012, and they would indeed have lost the state. But with Obama's experience in community organizing, looking at the election and the electorate in a fundamentally different way than the political class was accustomed to, he believed Florida was possible. When the question was put to him, he didn't blink, "We won it once, we can win it again."

Another factor, perhaps: Obama is extremely competitive, and only two Democratic presidents (Woodrow

Wilson and Franklin Roosevelt) have won Florida twice. He relished the opportunity to join them, especially because most of the political peanut gallery said it couldn't be done.

It could be done. Tens of thousands of volunteers worked their asses off for almost a year of seven-day weeks and registered a ton of new voters. We entered the stretch drive of the election with more than 130,000 more Democrats than Republicans.

Air Force One was on the ground nonstop in Florida at the end—as we approached Election day, you could see the momentum on the ground, and Obama became confident it would be in his column again based on his "feel" of what he was seeing. It's hard to describe, but a winning campaign with momentum at the end has a distinct, awesome feel.

We won with 50.01 percent of the vote, a 75,000-vote differential. Try to tell me the registration drive was not the difference.

So yes, registration matters. In our country, it is the necessary gateway to voting, which is the necessary gateway to winning, which is the necessary gateway to the change we seek. I agree it's a tragedy that we don't have automatic voter registration like Sweden has for eligible people, or even mandatory voting, like Australia has.

I understand that the battle to extend voting rights

freely to all citizens, of all colors, religions, genders, and so forth, has been one of our challenges for centuries. It's under relentless renewed attack right now by the GOP. But I'm also a rigorously pragmatic guy when it comes to winning elections. No whining about the electoral college and no whining about the voter registration laws. Let's change them when we can, but we have to win in 2020 under the weight of them right now.

You always want to play the game on the most favorable possible field, that is, the largest number of possible supporters. In political campaigns, there are only two ways to grow any candidate's numbers. One is convincing swing voters of the rightness of your cause. They're going to vote, and maybe they'll vote for you. The other is registering new voters who you think, based on a variety of data and demographic factors, will support your candidate or party. These folks aren't sure they're going to vote, but if they do, it will be for you.

Assuming you have a halfway decent candidate—and the Democrats will have a better candidate than that in 2020—I'm convinced that getting these might-vote people to the polls is actually the easiest path forward. Not that it's easy. It's hard, but persuading fence-sitters is even harder, in my opinion and experience.

Can we register every conceivable supporter, especially in battleground states, for the Democratic nominee? Of course not. But while perfection is impossible to achieve, that needs to be the goal, and first things first with the people who might vote: make sure they are properly registered and understand the rules of participation.

Consider this scenario. Let's say over the course of a sixty-day period, five thousand volunteers in Michigan were each responsible for just four new registrations. That's twenty thousand new Michigan voters, which is double the margin of votes by which Hillary Clinton lost Michigan last time. Each volunteer's five people might have turned the tide in 2016. That's how I ruefully look at it. Make sure your five are registered for 2020.

History has taught the Republicans some dangerous lessons they are trying to weaponize against Democrats and our democracy. The smaller the pie, the bigger their meal.

Their avowed goal is to make it as hard as possible to vote. Automatic voter registration in the blue states is awesome, but in the red states the Great Purge continues (see Georgia, 2018). Their strategies are infuriating and indefensible, but we have to fight our way through the land mines they are laying. The long-term solution is to maximize election reforms and protections in blue states and win back control in more red states. Then we can stop all these insidious efforts to make it harder to vote and actually change things to make it easier to vote. But in the meantime, we have an election we must win this year.

The potential voters are there, but all the money, all the data, all the grandiose ideas about what's possible as it relates to registration doesn't matter a whit without having the volunteer horsepower to get it done. Let's concentrate all our energy on creating a volunteer army of enough size, skill, and fortitude to reach the numbers we need. If you don't raise your hand to help, we're trapped in the world and the electorate as it is today—the one that produced President Trump.

So let's get to fashioning a new electorate, the best one possible.

First make sure you yourself are registered. Yeah, I know. You have that covered. But check. Go to a site like votesaveamerica.com to make sure all is proper, correct, and ready for 2020. If you have moved, inter- or intra-state, and have not changed your registration, *do it right now*! If you are a college student and a nonresident in a battleground state like Florida, Wisconsin, or Pennsylvania, register in that state.

This is your right, and you are spending most of your days there. You're sure your precinct voting location hasn't moved in twenty years? Confirm, please. Legion are the stories of veteran voters thrown for a loop on Election Day when it's no longer there. Most voters probably recover and vote a provisional ballot that gets counted later, but what if it's six thirty, the polls close at seven o'clock, and people throw up their hands? It happens.

Now what about your friends? I'm sure you think that everyone you know is registered and knows where to go, and you therefore want permission to skip this section.

Permission denied. I guarantee you're wrong. Somebody isn't correctly registered. Perhaps you can forget to check in with Uncle John if you are pretty sure that if he votes at all, he would pull the lever for Trump. Otherwise, make a comprehensive list of friends, family, neighbors, colleagues—especially if they've moved recently—and triple check that they are registered, and at the right address.

Posting your own confirmed status on Facebook is fine, and it may remind people to check theirs, but take the time to talk with them directly, whether it's the new person on your floor or your old gym friend. Some may roll their eyes or get annoyed at your obsessiveness, but if you are the reason just one or two people do register or reregister—well, it's just incredibly important. Feel free to be a pest.

But an educated pest. When someone in your immediate crowd has a question, be ready with the answer or at the least, be a source that can provide the answer. Take a few minutes to know the rules where you live. Where do you find these rules? Online, with voting-resource sites like brennancenter.org or log on to your local elections department or state Democratic Party websites.

Throughout the country, the registration laws are a patchwork, driven by state laws and practices. Fifteen states and the District of Columbia have now established automatic voter registration, though it's via the DMV, so all the potential voters without a driver's license are not automatically registered.

At least thirty-eight states have online registration. A few clicks and you're registered. More and more states are allowing seventeen-year-olds to preregister. They will be registered automatically when they turn eighteen. Twenty-one states, including Wisconsin—Wisconsin!—have same-day voter registration, meaning you can register and vote on Election Day. To be superefficient, though, I would encourage you to get registered earlier. Some jurisdictions allow you to become a permanent absentee or mail-in voter at the time you register to vote.

If it all sounds complicated when you look across state lines, it is. One simple standard would be awesome. But you only have to worry about your state. So that's simple.

Now it's time to extend your reach and up your game! Once you've confirmed everyone in your family and social circle and softball team and pottery class is registered, it's time to consider a wider impact. And I have great news. There are a lot of different ways to bring in voters eligible to depose Trump, so you may want to join existing groups or efforts.

Your local Democratic Party, community groups, national groups like the NAACP, Indivisible, and Next-Gen will be deep into registration efforts. Check sites like mobilizeamerica.io for local groups looking for volunteer help to register voters. They'll put you to work. You'll probably go through a short training session or be assigned a seasoned registrar to work with the first time, depending on the state. At any given time, they may be running a campaign at a block party, a shopping mall or local festival. You might be asked to sit in a booth at an event and help registrants with the forms. You might even be asked to walk around a neighborhood, canvassing, hitting doors of the unregistered.

Or bite the bullet and strike out on your own, perhaps with some friends. Set up a table at popular local events, or a private party. And don't worry about whether you will get traffic. You set up a card table with a sign that says, "Want to Beat Trump?" and people will stop. Oh, they will most definitely stop. But there's a lot more to it than that. You're taking on a big responsibility, and you have to see it through. You may need permission first, so contact the site where you want to set up shop. Be prepared with paperwork—you need voter registration forms, obtained from—well, you have to know where. Know all the rules in your state, and make sure it's a state that allows you even to work as an agent helping people fill out forms on the spot and delivering them to local election officials. If you can't be an agent, simply have forms available for people to complete and turn in themselves, and have cards ready to hand out telling them where to send or turn in the forms. Maybe you want to spring for prestamped preaddressed envelopes. Also have a laptop available with internet or a smartphone so that people can check their registration status, sign up to register on the spot, and check the current location of their polling places.

Obviously, if you're working for an organization, those good people will probably gather the registration forms and file them for you. They'll provide other support. But however you proceed, I can't say it too often: never doubt how your individual effort can make a profound difference. Even more so if it gets others to act. Always be ready with information for people who stop by and want to volunteer to defeat our racist president.

Which leads into. . . .

Storytelling. As encouraged at length in the preceding chapter, amplify all that you are doing. Changing your registration because you moved? Take a picture and post it on Instagram. Going door-to-door registering voters?

Do a quick Facebook live between doors, especially after you've registered someone, capturing how the experience makes you feel. Working a community event? Capture through picture, video, or word the experience and link to how people can join you. Is there a neighborhood newsletter or block organization that might cover your efforts?

Is there a local TV station that needs content, such as you talking to students at the local high school? In the fractured media and information environment, you simply never know when you will reach an important target voter or potential volunteer, or when your simple tweet will get retweeted by someone with ten times your followers. That's the upside of our hypernetworked social media world—use it!

If enough of you are doing your own individual storytelling about the import, means, and activities to increase voter registration, the frequency and intensity will both reach people we need to register as well as motivate others to volunteer, then all of a sudden you reach the scale you need in your precinct and state and that we need in our country.

It also just feels damn good to help people participate in their democracy at a time when the white patriarchy would like to make it harder for people who don't look and think like them simply to exercise their franchise.

Registering won't get you to victory if our people don't then vote. Much has rightly been written about some of the challenges the Democratic turnout operations faced in places like Detroit and Milwaukee in 2016. In 2020, our GOTV (Get out the Vote) operation has to be better. This critical issue receives a chapter of its own later, but we have to start here, at the most fundamental level: registering citizens who will vote to Dump Trump if we get them to take the first step of becoming eligible.

4

HOSTING

★ ★ ★

Much—OK, most—of this presidential campaign will be waged with smartphones and computers, with people engaging with their devices at home, in the workplace, even on the street. That's a lot of screens and a lot of media, social and otherwise. Digital detox is important in life—I know when I am away from my phone for even a couple of hours it seems like a three-day vacation. It's important in politics too.

Everyone could use a break now and then. So get together with your campaign friends and colleagues in person. Throw a house or apartment party. It's a homely subject, I admit, but it would be hard to exaggerate its importance.

In the Obama campaign in 2008, we broke new technological ground with our national house parties. Then-Senator Obama appeared via a livestream on computers in homes throughout the country. There were some technical glitches, and that technology now seems prehistoric, but our people loved the parties. It's something we carried forward in both campaigns, and most important, our volunteers carried forward on their own. No command and control needed.

There is just no doubt that these parties really create a sense of shared purpose and a comforting conviction that together you can get all the work done, and win.

In 2020, the candidate and you will use the very latest streaming possibilities. I can imagine our nominee appearing at the house parties by hologram—a technology I believe was first used in political campaigns by India's prime minister Narendra Modi in 2014.

Of course you do not have to wait for the national campaign to organize your own house parties—and may I suggest that an excellent time for your first party is right after the primaries are over and we finally know who our candidate will be. Bring together a range of friends, families, and acquaintances, good Democrats all who will have supported different candidates over the preceding months. For those whose choice or choices didn't prevail, take a moment to console yourselves, remember the highlights of your adventures, brainstorm about how everyone will now shift gears and build and strengthen the local organization for our nominee.

For those of you who were with the winner all along, listen and learn from those who were on the other side. Losing isn't easy. People usually don't respond well to, "OK, we won, you lost, now let's all get in line."

Let them process and let them add to where your campaign in the primary was weak.

And speak your mind if you were on the losing side of the primary. If you supported a candidate who had outsized appeal with certain sectors in your community—maybe younger voters or blue-collar men or college-educated women—you need to talk about your attraction to your candidate in the first place and explain how you will use that passion and knowledge to try to create and maintain support and enthusiasm for the winning candidate in those important segments of the Democratic constituency.

This is the time to have every single voter acknowledge that the prelims are over, and now we have one and only one opponent: Donald Trump. We need everyone who worked in the primaries to throw themselves into the general election campaign with full force. Nothing else should distract us, not old differences, old grievances, nothing.

I hope this won't be too hard, not in 2020.

I experienced firsthand the importance of this healing and uniting process following the Obama-Clinton primary in 2008. That was a rough battle—much rougher than the Clinton-Sanders primary in 2016. In the aftermath, our campaign didn't do everything right to bring the sides together, but our principal did, and so did Senator Clinton. They set the right tone so that those of us at the staff level could follow their lead, though it was admittedly really difficult to just drop the weaponry one day and pretend we were all one happy family the next.

Primaries are often more intense than general elections in the lingering hard feelings they produce. There are still older Democrats throughout the country who identify as Carter or Kennedy followers, just like there are younger voters who are Obama or Clinton Dems. These are family disputes, always the rawest kind, and while our candidates in the primaries have differences on issues, they share much more common ground than not. The key differentiators are therefore more personal—character, style, background, performance, age. Those distinctions create much more heat and passion than Democrats versus Republicans on issues, which are now, profoundly and sadly, already baked into the cake.

In 2008, postprimaries, time was of the essence, and we had to unite. The general election was only five months away. Beating John McCain was not going to be easy. The political oddsmakers had it at 50-50.

Hoping to bridge any divide, I attended any number of events with passionate Clinton supporters. I soon learned that the less I said, the better. Let Clinton's supporters vent about some of the things said or done during the primary that they thought had been unfair. Let them express their unease about truly being welcomed by the Obama forces in their city or community. Share their concerns about Obama's ability to win. Share their disappointment that Clinton was not going to be on the ticket as the VP, which we made clear early in that search process.

Where I had something meaningful to say or could allay concerns, I tried, but largely these sessions became opportunities for the losing candidate's supporters to process everything with one another—and occasionally direct their shared frustration at me. By the end of this outreach, we had laid the foundation for most of them to join in common cause with Obama supporters to focus on the shared goal of winning back the presidency.

In 2020, given the lengthy list of viable candidates, a great deal of such processing could be necessary among the official campaign workers and their volunteer supporters at your house party, and this can be the most effective catalyst for turning the page. Conversations among a bunch of committed Democrats in your cozy home will be far more effective, candid, and welcoming than social media exchanges, where it's all too easy to take potshots or chew on lingering recriminations and real and perceived outrages from the primary. It's a lot harder to hate up close. Hosting and attending postprimary events can be incredibly important to uniting our Democratic family and moving forward en masse.

The obvious opportunity for your next house party is the convention in Milwaukee in mid-July. Back as recently as 1968, conventions were consumed with backroom, brass-knuckle wheeling and dealing to select the candidate. There was lots of drama about what would happen and how. And who would do what to whom.

These days conventions are as close to a free throw as you get in politics. Not much breaking news. Really hard to screw up. Clint Eastwood and the empty chair at Romney's convention in 2012 being a notable exception to that rule.

But this is also the great thing about watching one of these modern conventions with a bunch of people. The terrific parts carry their own water—this year, the Obamas' speeches will be must-see TV, as will those from the nominee's spouse, VP pick, and of course the star of the show, our next president.

And there can always be surprises. Remember, it was

at John Kerry's coronation in Boston in 2004 that most of the country caught its first glimpse of the powerful oratory of one Barack Obama, and this year one or more of our rebuilding farm team could likewise startle the nation from the podium in Milwaukee. And all the less compelling speakers and the boilerplate stuff? They give your guests a good opportunity to imbibe, nosh, and exchange wisecracks and get closer as a team.

With such a crowd, watching the convention should not be an angst ridden, looking-between-your-fingers-at-the-big screen-TV experience. It should be inspirational, motivational, and clarifying, and make you proud of our party and our nominee. Now, in the unlikely event the primary contest continues all the way to this convention, with the result up in the air, well, that will be a different TV show altogether, and a different house party, and reconciliation and unification will be harder, more urgent, and with far less time to pull off.

And hosting a crowd to watch Trump's shitshow of a convention? It certainly won't be inspiring, but it will be searingly motivational and clarifying. The America they all talk about in Charlotte will be foreign to you and me. If it doesn't fire you up to do everything within your power to wipe Trump off the face of the political earth, I'm not sure anything can. It's a good moment to make sure everyone in attendance is signed up to volunteer and financially contribute if they can. Pass around the laptop and ask those that aren't to get with the program.

Next on the house party calendars around the country could be the debates. Your candidate's strong performance when you're watching with a crowd can provide a real shot in the arm for everyone. It's not much different from the joy of watching your favorite sports team win an important game surrounded by your friends and family.

And when it's not going so well in the debate hall, it can induce a lot of concern, panic, yelling at the screen, and even fatalistic reaction. It's a good reason why you should not watch alone or even with just your nuclear family. There is strength in numbers and, if necessary, comfort as well. It definitely was in the first reelection debate with Mitt Romney in 2012. This was the evening when President Obama seemed marooned somewhere between boredom with the whole thing—detached and distracted—and just plain irritated. We who had prepped him for the debate had clearly done a piss-poor job as well.

The pundits' reviews were universally bad. Many suggested we had thrown out the window not just our modest but steady lead over Romney but the entire election. Voters' reviews were no more kind.

Many of you watched those debates with your fellow Obama supporters and volunteers. I spent that night—all night, if I recall—with my colleagues in a crowded conference room in our hotel in the suburbs of Denver, trying to diagnose what had gone wrong, how to fix it, and most pressingly important, how to get off the mat only eight hours later. Basically, how to say a bunch of the stuff we should have said in the debate, without it seeming not a total mea culpa. Though for the most part it was.

The president had events in Colorado and Wisconsin the next day before heading back to the White House, and we actually had a decent and pretty feisty day after: Obama, with gusto and relish, prosecuted Romney for lying through his teeth about his record and plans. Still, the coverage of these pretty good events was understandably still being viewed through the prism of the debate: "Where was this Obama last night? That Obama was petulant, professorial, and missing opportunities."

What are the five stages of grief in presidential politics? Shock, defiance, regret, gallows humor, and finally optimism that we would get our mojo back. That last one was a bit forced and hopeful at three a.m., but it turned out to be true. In the following days, it was incredibly helpful to me and my colleagues to process the debacle with one another. I can't imagine you, the committed

Obama supporter, turning on your TV and watching that debate alone, or even with spouse or kids. You're thinking, "This seems really bad—but maybe it's not as bad I think." Then the commentary starts pouring in, and it universally judges the performance as even worse than you thought. Was Andrew Sullivan right? Had Obama thrown away the presidency in those ninety fateful minutes? Just about everyone agreed that he might have. And in the middle of all this negativity you're alone or close to it, maybe texting a friend or two for comfort? Sounds miserable. Much better to be with a group. You could vent. "Why was Obama so bad? "I've never seen him like that!" "Why did he keep looking down and looking annoyed when Romney was talking?" "Plouffe and Axelrod don't know what the hell they are doing."

All warranted. Then you could turn to your friends and guests, discuss the ramifications, calmly and rationally, and hopefully work through things with the others. "Well, he had a huge lead after Romney's 47 percent gaffe. He can afford to lose a point or two." "There was no way he was going to win as big as the polls were saying. Tonight probably just accelerates Romney's comeback, which was going to happen anyway." "As long as he shows up in the next two like we know he can, it'll be OK." "Yeah, this is the first time he hasn't delivered at a big moment. He'll get the next two." "Totally. There is no way he can be that bad two more times."

Whatever it takes. Then the discussion most likely moves to what's next. "Well, the race is going to tighten up, so we all better do more volunteering than we were planning on." "I doubt he'll bomb again in the next debate, but we better get out there and do all we can to lock in support now." "We better mix things up for the next one—I'll host." Superstition around debates is always appreciated. After we did indeed recover in the second debate, some of us took it to an extreme for the third and final debate, insisting on eating the same food that day and wearing the same clothes as we did for the second. Please feel free to employ your own superstitious behaviors as needed!

Wouldn't that be much better to soften the blow than fretting alone? Working through everything with a group, maybe you would not have slept much better, perhaps a little, but you'd certainly have woken up with a bit more perspective and resolve.

Best of all for all your volunteers in the country? Be good in the debates! That's a lot more fun and gratifying for the candidate, the campaign team, and all the volunteers watching around the country. In his six general election debates, Obama went 5–1. So despite our one wretched bomb, we provided some highlights and momentum in the other five. Those are great memories. It's also just simply nice, after all the hard work you are putting in, to sit back for ninety minutes and watch the main event together with your fellow travelers and spend some time processing and socializing before and after. In any election, it's important to be reminded together of the stakes and the differences between the candidates, to reaffirm why winning is so important, and to talk afterward about what else each of us can do to get our candidate across the finish line.

In 2020, we will be reminded just about every hour by our president's offensive and dumb tweets. The three debates are opportunities to see the Orange Menace and our candidate side by side, a perfect comparison. They'll be the perfect reminder of how close we are to electing a sane, good, smart, and well-meaning president (not to mention all the issue and policy differences). For the supporters gathered around your little campfire, could it be more motivating, reassuring, and powerful?

Homely it may be, but once you put your creativity to hosting, the opportunities are endless. Live in a rural community that's been gutted by Trump's crazy tariff wars? Invite a few farmers or small business owners to go to the town square or local diner to talk about how Trump has screwed up their livelihood with taxes, or embargoes, or labor practices. Invite the local paper, local radio station, or the neighborhood blogger to cover the festivities. If they don't make it, include them on the list of recipients receiving your own video. Or livestream it yourself on YouTube. Don't wait for the nominee's campaign people to organize an event like this—they may never get to it. Take it into your own hands.

And don't just gather your friends and neighbors; think about all those out of towners who've come to help out in your community. Those of you who live in a battleground state will have field organizers from the nominee's campaign camping out (sometimes literally) in your community or close to it. Outside a battleground state, you might have campaign staff temporarily living nearby helping raise money or recruit volunteers. It would be great if you could invite these folks over for a late dinner, hang out a bit, maybe watch a sporting event or show together—and they'll also have to listen to your ideas for the campaign and tips about the local scene. If they're really good at their job, they'll be as hungry to hear them as they are for the home-cooked meal

I'm sure I am biased, or at least affected, by the many years I spent as a campaign staffer in Delaware, Iowa, Wisconsin, Massachusetts, New Jersey, and Illinois (and traveling to every state but North Dakota and Alaska), where I learned that hosting one-on-one like this will make a huge difference in a staffer's morale. Particularly in the beginning of my career, those of us in the Democratic trenches didn't have money to eat out anywhere decent or any time to cook, much less go to the grocery store. Food was on the fly, a gas station burrito here, a 7-Eleven hot dog there, a doughnut and a Slim Jim getting us by.

We didn't know many people in the communities we moved to. Our apartments probably didn't have TV, and we certainly didn't have laptops, and there was no Netflix to stream for a few minutes before falling asleep on a lumpy mattress and doing it all over again the next day. Maybe a beat-up paperback of *Fear and Loathing on The Campaign Trail '72* to keep you company. Wages have improved a bit over the last generation, but the life is still pretty spartan. Field organizers aren't doing it for the money, but still it's hard and lonely, and you can get really hungry.

Extending an invite to your local campaign staffer to break bread with your family, play with your kids, or watch something together may not seem like much, but to a broke, tired, unhealthy campaign staffer, your split-level ranch will seem like a luxury spa. Of course, they'll feel and probably say they don't have time. Cajole them until they assent to your generous invite.

Morale is important. Just make sure that you plan ahead for seconds and thirds at the table and excuse the pace at which your guests eat. Your meal will probably be the best and most food they've had in months. Make this banquet a weekly occurrence, and you may just be responsible for that staffer's performance at an even higher level. You may make a lifelong friend. When I went to Iowa in frigid early January to celebrate and mark the ten-year anniversary of Obama's caucus victory with much of the original Iowa campaign team, it warmed me up to hear many of the former organizers talking about the local precinct leaders and volunteers they still stayed in close touch with, even though for some of them this event was the first time they had set foot back in the state in ten years. When you go through a crucible together, the ties that bind are unique and long lasting.

BATTLEGROUNDS

★ ★ ★

I t's a term you'll hear me and everyone else remotely connected to any presidential campaign use over and over—battleground states. And if it already feels battle worn, it's worn out for a reason. Blame it on the Founding Fathers and our Constitution.

To win the presidency, you have to win the vote in the electoral college. The popular vote (total votes cast throughout the nation) is interesting, but as we learned in 2016, it's almost irrelevant in the presidential election. There are no more important considerations than mounting a campaign strong enough to win enough of individual states to get to 270 electoral college votes.

Because of this, in a presidential campaign, you can sometimes feel like you're running super-sized governor's races in a few states more than you are a national campaign. You know ahead of time that some states are rigidly red, and others are truest blue; you pretty much know whether you can count on them to vote your way when the electoral college meets. While you can't ignore any of them, the real battle is fought in the rest, what we now call the purple states.

So what is the cleanest definition of a battleground state? A state whose electoral votes really are up for grabs in a particular election. In true landslide presidential elections—the last one was George H. W. Bush's in 1988—the electoral college results are so lopsided that no states could be identified as the ones whose narrow margins of victory could have gone either way and made all the difference. The winner wins just about all of them.

There will not be an electoral landslide in 2020. The battlegrounds will be the difference, just as they were in 2016. We could think of them as the tipping points in this election. They could swing either way. They're the states that happen to make our close divisions as a society manifest for all to see. Eke out a victory over your opponent in enough of them in 2020 and become president of the United States. Or remain as president for four more years. How they fall will decide so much of our country's fate in the coming years and decades. It can't get more important than this.

In 2020, there are five, maybe six for sure. That's all. There could be more—say Texas and Georgia become targets for the Democrat, and New Hampshire and Nevada for Trump. But these won't be the tipping-point states–their 270th electoral vote– but they would be cushions: their 300th or 330th electoral votes. Let's say there are four to six states that won't be tipping-point states, but one or both candidates will decide to contest.

The other thirty-eight to forty states are done deals for one candidate or the other. Some (Hawaii or Mississippi) will be blowouts—sixty to forty or even wider for one of the candidates. The popular vote breakdown in some other states (South Carolina or New Mexico) might look relatively sort of close—say, 55 to 45 percent—but the losing side has no actual chance of getting to a win number in that state. Close doesn't count in the electoral college. You get zero electoral college votes for losing narrowly. And if you lost the college narrowly—well, as they say, close only counts in horseshoes and hand grenades. Only great pain comes from coming close.

I want you to have a little historical background with which to wow your friends at your next campaign house party. The battleground map in 2020 isn't going to change much from 2016, but the electoral map has changed immensely over the decades. It's not static. When you look at historical electoral college results maps on sites like

270towin.com, this reality is shockingly stark. One comparison says it all: in 1976—eleven elections ago—Republican president Gerald Ford (after taking over from the deposed Richard Nixon) comfortably won states like California, Vermont, and Washington, all bright blue states today. Democratic challenger (and winner) Jimmy Carter comfortably won West Virginia, Tennessee, and Kentucky, all rock-solid red states today. And you can take this to the bank: the battleground map in 2064—eleven elections from now—will barely resemble ours this year. States will transition from blue to purple (that is, battleground status) to red and then back to blue. A lot of this movement will be driven by demographics. In 2018, Beto O'Rourke, running for Senate against Ted Cruz and coming pretty close, showed that it's just a question of when, not if, Texas becomes a battleground state. So that's good news.

If you ponder more recent elections, the role and definition of battleground states comes into sharp focus. In 2000, Al Gore lost Florida by 538 votes, 538 votes that made the difference between a war and no war in Iraq, accelerating climate change versus fighting it. In 2004, George Bush had a healthy national popular vote lead, but Kerry came within 100,000 votes of winning the presidency.

The culprit was one state, Ohio, and Kerry's campaign

hit their number—they secured the total number of votes they thought it would take to win the Buckeye State, based on sound turnout estimates. What happened? Something we should fear this time as well—the Bush campaign pulled off one of the more miraculous feats in recent elections, building an organization in Ohio strong and deep enough to find, register, and turn out conservative voters in numbers few thought were possible. Kerry's sure-bet figures did not keep up.

With the 2000 and 2004 outcomes freshly in mind, the Obama campaigns of 2008 and 2012 were bound and determined not to allow it to come down to one state again. Because of Obama's appeal and strength as a candidate, our passionate and motivated volunteers, and abundant financial resources, we decided to put new states in play, including some the Democrats had written off or not contested in a long time. We wanted a large number of states in play, playing more offense than defense, giving us a much higher (that is, safer) margin for error. We prepared for exceedingly close races that could come down to a vote or two per precinct, razor-thin margins of victory and defeat. We could lose many of the states we, if not many other people, considered battlegrounds and still win the presidency.

In 2008, our core battleground target list was therefore a long one: Nevada, Colorado, Montana, Missouri,

Iowa, Pennsylvania, Wisconsin, New Hampshire, Ohio, Indiana, Virginia, North Carolina and Florida. (And don't forget the second congressional district of Nebraska, which joins Maine in awarding electoral college votes to the winner of individual congressional districts as well as to the statewide winning candidate.) Michigan, traditionally a battleground in this era, was conceded early by McCain, in a move that showed just how narrow McCain's win path was becoming. They pulled out in September, and we ended up winning that traditional battleground by 15 points.

Our strategy worked. Fourteen battleground states, and we won all but two, Montana and Missouri, and even won the 2nd Congressional District of Nebraska, winning one Husker electoral college vote while losing the state.

That gave our first African American president 365 electoral votes (270 required to win). In the electoral college at least, a landslide. We won 67.8 percent of the electoral college while winning 52.9 percent of the popular vote. That's what happens when you come close to sweeping all the battlegrounds.

By the way, I'm still royally pissed about the two that got away. I desperately wanted to color all of those states Obama blue. The battlegrounds become like children to a campaign manager, all precious in their own way, and you want them to be taken care of and come home to where they belong.

In 2012, we knew we were going to face a stiffer challenge and closer race than in 2008 due to an economy still recovering from the financial crisis four years earlier. Once again we believed we had to widen the playing field to put pressure on Mitt Romney to compete in as many theaters of political battle as possible, thus preserving a healthy margin of error for ourselves. Our core battleground list was smaller than the huge one in 2008, but still historically large: Nevada, Colorado, Iowa, Pennsylvania, New Hampshire, Virginia, North Carolina, and Florida. Michigan? In fits and starts, the Romney campaign claimed that it would contest things up there, making it a quasi battleground, I suppose, but there was little doubt in our minds (and more important, in our data) that the Wolverine State would be safely Obama blue again.

We won all of those battleground targets save for North Carolina, and yes, that outlier still rankles. President Obama secured reelection with 332 electoral votes. And there was no more important factor in that decisive victory—in both of them, when we outperformed our national popular vote margins in the battlegrounds—than our amazing volunteers who stretched what was possible for us through registration, turnout, and persuasion.

In 2016? A much different story. Trump won 306

electoral college votes on Election Night, 56.8 percent of them. While, as we all know too well, winning only 46.1 percent of the national popular vote. Which was a lower vote total than Romney received when he lost the electoral college decisively. Give this to the Trump campaign: they squeezed out every electoral college vote they could from their paltry national numbers.

Now we are near 2020's campaign, and I can say with certainty that for us to have any chance of beating Trump in 2020, we will need even more effort from you, the volunteers, than we saw in 2008, 2012, and 2018.

There's no time to waste moaning about everything that brought us to this crossroads. Obama demonstrated, quite recently, that we can win more than enough to tip battlegrounds over in the electoral college. The volunteers will be the key ingredient, and we will have a fight on our hands in that regard because Trump has large numbers of fiercely committed volunteers.

I'm not sure bragging that you could murder someone on Fifth Avenue without losing any votes is something to actually brag about, but to his base this is rock solid truth. I suspect Trump will come close to maxing out Republican turnout, which could be scarily high, meaning we have to match it and then some. The MAGA gang is not turning over the keys to the White House to the Democratic Party—that socialist hoard that believes

everyone should have access to affordable health care—
without an epic fight.

About a year before the election, as I'm writing
this chapter, everyone is already focused on Michigan,
Pennsylvania, and Wisconsin as the three critical battlegrounds. These three were supposed to compose the
"blue wall" that the Democrats could count on last time,
but the wall crumbled, Hillary Clinton lost all of them,
and here we are today, trapped in the rubble.

In 2020, those states will be political war zones. Add
them to the twenty states plus the District of Columbia
that Clinton did collect and our nominee wins with 272
electoral votes. The contest for the presidency may come
down to block-by-block street fights in Detroit, Philadelphia, and Milwaukee.

However, we definitely don't want the election to
come down to a contest in only three states. That gives
us a zero margin for error and takes far too much for
granted about actual turnout in the so-called safe states.
We win only two of those three states and we still lose.
Definitely not OK.

We need to play offense elsewhere, expand the map,
as the Obama campaign did in 2008, especially. Almost certainly, our nominee will target Florida. Win
those 29 electoral votes (Obama did it twice, narrowly)
and Trump's odds slip to precarious levels. With Florida

in the blue column, we'd only have to win one of the three core midwestern battlegrounds.

Some analysts believe Florida is already lost. Bullshit in my view. Hillary lost it by less than a percentage point, and Democrats Andrew Gillum and Bill Nelson narrowly lost their 2018 races for governor and senator, respectively. Note all the "narrowlys," and of course Al Gore was a whisker away from winning in 2000. The battleground map does change from cycle to cycle, but one constant for almost a generation has been the Sunshine State—always a battleground and superclose at that. And let's not forget North Carolina. The Democratic nominee has to look hard at North Carolina, a state Barack Obama narrowly won once and narrowly lost once. Although Hillary Clinton lost the state in 2016, the state still elected a Democrat that same year. North Carolina offers a significant fifteen electoral votes. I hope it's firmly in the battleground state mix.

And an exciting, new core battleground entrant is likely to be Arizona, where Clinton came closer in 2016 than Obama did in either of his races. She lost the Grand Canyon State less than she lost Iowa and Ohio. The whisker Gore lost by in Florida was the whisker Kyrsten Sinema won by in a Senate race in 2018, and Democrats showed down-ballot strength throughout the state. Arizona is shifting demographically, with Latino voters becoming a more powerful force and suburban voters trending more and more Democratic. Win Arizona and its 11 electoral votes, add wins in Pennsylvania and Michigan, and our nominee can lose Wisconsin and Florida and we'll win. That's the math to remember.

And what a night to remember that would be, watching one Donald J. Trump deliver his concession speech on Election Night. Wouldn't that be an amazing, amazing pleasure? What a motivation.

Or, in a fit of rage and denial, he doesn't concede. I'll take that too, as historically narcissistic and petty as it would be. Grace notes? Not how our current President rolls.

If the economy weakens in the year before the election, more states could easily be deemed authentic battlegrounds by the Democrat. Or once battlegrounds turn into safer Democratic territory. This happened very late in 2008, following the collapse of Lehman Bros. on Wall Street on September 15.

In 2020, Ohio and Iowa would be the most likely late-arriving battlegrounds. Both are still quasi competitive, so a weakening economy should make them full-blown competitive.

Georgia, believe it or not, may be a top target as well. It would take a herculean effort by the volunteers in the state to put together a winning coalition, but Stacey Abrams showed us the way with that narrowest of losses in her stirring gubernatorial race in 2018. The troops are waiting to charge if HQ decides to open up the Georgia front. And if it doesn't? I've said it before and I'll say it again: you don't have to wait for the campaign. Good things will come up and down the ballot.

Defensively, Democrats need to watch Minnesota carefully. Clinton won it by only 2 points, and it shares many demographic characteristics with its neighbors to the immediate east and south, Wisconsin and Iowa, which fell to Trump; it would be surprising if the Trump campaign doesn't decide to make an all-out effort in the Land of 10,000 Lakes. They could also try to win Maine statewide (they won the northern congressional district in 2020, garnering one electoral vote), and they may decide to make a stand in New Hampshire and Nevada, if only to annoy us and drain some resources. It's a chess match of sorts. Nobody has a bottomless war chest of resources, and decisions about where to direct time, money, and people are not made in a vacuum. If we're pretty confident about a state, Nevada, say, in our case, but the Trump campaign decides to push hard, well, we can't let them run completely scot-free and risk turning our steady 2-point lead into a dangerous dead heat.

In any presidential campaign, the battleground states suck up the lion's share of the dollars—a subject I'll return to in the following short chapter—but the most important currency in the battle for the battlegrounds is not money or campaign staff or even the candidate's own time. It's you and your time. I believe a successful presidential campaign is built on healthy connective tissue that runs from the candidate all the way down to the high schooler stuffing envelopes. It includes a presidential nominee who builds and inspires a talented and motivated staff; a staff in turn who recruits, inspires, and believes in strong local volunteer leaders; staff and volunteer leaders who welcome, train, listen to, and believe in volunteers; and volunteers who motivate, give strength to, and make the impossible possible for the candidate. Another virtuous circle in presidential campaign politics.

Given how close the battleground states have historically been and will definitely be again in 2020, your effort and those of your fellow committed citizens can flat out be determinative. What if in 2016 in Wisconsin the Clinton campaign had done all they could from HQ to win it and that effort was matched by a ferocious, well-supported volunteer effort? Well, I think we know. But that's hindsight, which is worthless. We made mistakes in the Obama campaign despite our victories and no doubt our nominee in 2020 will as well.

The point is we need close to a perfect campaign to be run by the campaign professionals matched with a large-scale, effective, and intensive volunteer effort in the core battlegrounds. One won't matter without the other.

Let's dig into the battleground states. Some of you volunteers will be in residence while others will be pitching in from afar (which might not be very afar, maybe right across the state line).

Let's start this discussion with those of you who do live in a battleground state (or have long desired to, in which case there's no time like the present to finally make the move!) The first thing you want to do is let the campaign know that you exist and are interested in volunteering. You can easily do this through the candidate's website. You raising your hand will be shared—in close to real time, I hope—with the staff and volunteer leaders who are already in place in your area. They'll contact you. Make clear to them that you intend to be part of a winning effort. If you don't hear back, and there's an office address listed, just drop in. If they're shorthanded, you might quickly get enrolled to start replying to other volunteers' inquiries.

Be prepared to tell them what you can contribute. Think about this before you check in. What are you great at and like doing? Making posters? Cooking food for the other volunteers? Phone calling? Door knocking? Signing in people at events? Data entry? Can you help feed and house volunteers coming in from out of state? Do you drive and do you have a car? The point is we need help not doing just one thing, but a whole lot of things, by a whole lot of people to make this all work.

An important point that may not be self-evident: a campaign will make targeting and resource decisions based in part on the strength of the organization that they anticipate they can muster at both the state and precinct level. So signing up early signals to the powers that be in the campaign that they should deploy resources to your community. This is what you want, because you want to win.

If your time is limited or your availability fluctuates week to week, say so. Every hour counts, every task is vital—housing other volunteers, driving them around, driving voters to polls, the list is endless, really. And be realistic in your appraisal of your availability. Do all you can, but don't overpromise. It's not as if, after volunteering, you will magically have fewer work and family obligations.

Do all that you can, but be realistic and honest about how much of all that there can be.

In an election of this magnitude, when the only way we will win is with enough volunteer activity in certain states, many of us throughout the country—and the world—will be counting on you. Don't add to that pressure by signing up or signaling you can do more than you can.

Speaking of pressure, the pressure on any presidential candidate is enormous. The pressures on the Democratic nominee in 2020 to rid us of the scourge of Trump?

The weight the candidate will feel, the obligation, the unrelenting pressure—I really don't believe the rest of us can properly imagine it.

Aside from the confidence you can provide those of us outside the battlegrounds that you are taking care of business, you should know you are providing comfort to our nominee, making her or him perform better and become a stronger candidate. I want to buttress this important point with a couple of stories from the 2012 reelection campaign.

After President Obama's horrid first debate that year with Romney in Colorado—his first time in the ring with that opponent—after he had finally and totally accepted the scale of our defeat, his major observation to me in the Oval Office a couple of days after the debate was his disappointment in letting all of his grassroots supporters down. This was what he felt worst about. I don't remember his exact words, but in essence he said, "Everyone's out there working their hearts out, and now I've made it harder for them. I'm sure I've disappointed them as well. I care more about not doing that again even more than winning."

Now, that sounds like an implausible line, written by Aaron Sorkin for President Bartlet in *The West Wing*. But it's true and not a unique attitude for the man. Time after time, when we hit rocky shoals during those nine years, his biggest concern was how his volunteers would react.

They really were his North Stars, the most important people in his political universe, and I think they understood this. It was an incredibly powerful connection, which was brought home to me in even starker relief a few days after the Oval Office conversation. We had decamped to the Homestead, a resort in central Virginia, to hold a three-day debate camp to prep for the second debate, to be held at Hofstra on Long Island.

Candidate Obama was much more dialed in this time, as were we all, hoping that the first debate had been nothing more than a probationary moment, if a dangerous one. The major impact was probably an acceleration of the movement back to Romney by voters who were always going to end up there by Election Day, but we couldn't afford two lemons in a row.

At debate prep camp, candidates may take a break and go out and hold one event nearby in order to generate some press and social media activity and not be "dark" (no media coverage) for three full days. We suggested, and Obama readily agreed, that our one outing outside the camp's confines would be to the campaign office near Williamsburg, Virginia, to meet with local volunteers and thank them for all they were doing.

While we felt pretty confident about keeping Virginia in our column, Romney was mounting a fierce challenge. It was going to be relatively close. We could not be too overconfident. After all, in 2008, Obama had been the first Democrat since LBJ to win the state.

A necessary quick flashback: for the first debate, the camp was held outside Las Vegas. We Obama staffers had not put much of a premium on these excursions in 2008, and neither had Obama. Four years later in Nevada, however, he kept pushing us to come up with ideas for cool things to do. In the end we toured Hoover Dam, which is an awesome place and was an awesome experience for him and those who went, generating some great photos. He was like a teenager wanting to get out of the house and clearly had a grand time for those hours, a much grander time than while actually prepping, with all of us staffers nitpicking his lame prep work with our own lame advice. It's no surprise that his parting words to David Axelrod and me before he jumped on stage for the first debate, was a desultory "Let's get this over with."

Like going to the dentist for a filling, and it showed.

Now, back to the local headquarters in eastern Virginia during the second debate prep camp.

Obama brought pizza, laughed, hugged, listened, made some phone calls himself to voters, thanked and, I'm sure, motivated the couple dozen volunteers on hand whose work, multiplied throughout the fifty states, was going to determine whether he would be a one- or two-term president.

I know for sure these local volunteers in Virginia motivated the president because when he got back to the resort and we were getting ready for that night's mock debate—a full ninety-minute sparring session with John Kerry, who had graciously agreed to inhabit and play the role of Mitt Romney, the Republican challenger in 2012—our man was full of clarity and purpose. He also said to me, "I was kind of nervous going to the office, because I just feel like I let them all down. But to a person, they said they had my back and they'd been working harder since the first debate. I told them I wouldn't let them down in the second debate. They all said, 'You better not!'"

You may not have a similar face-to-face with our nominee, though if you live in a battleground state, there is a fair chance you will meet the boss. But understand that it's not just the registration numbers you are putting up that matter. It's your spirit and commitment that are the real wind beneath the candidate's wings.

Obama went on to convincingly win the second debate, even more so the third debate, then he decisively won on election night and earned the right to continue steering our national ship in a progressive direction. I am convinced that the trip to the local campaign office played no small part in our getting off the mat and turning the corner after the first debate. Those volunteers motivated him, inspired him, and he had them in mind when he took that debate stage in New York and beyond. And, by the way, we carried Virginia. Again.

If you live in a battleground state, you have a front row seat to history. But why not leave the stands, jump on the field, and help *make* that history? If your state is called for Trump and lights up red on the big TV maps, the one thing I'm sure you don't want to feel is that there was more you could have done.

One decision to make right now, as you game out the level and intensity of your involvement, is whether you have the time and are willing to develop the skills to play the critical role of neighborhood leader or precinct captain. Accepting this responsibility means you will meet some awesome people, all bound together by a common cause, convinced that our country can be better, must be better, and good people of all kinds need to make it so.

Can one election really signify all that? You tell me. Tell me how you will feel on election night if that child-like sociopath in the White House is empowered to give another victory speech, his hatred and misogyny and racism ratified for another four years, or if his second inaugural address infects your phones and computers, your kids, our country and our world, and promises four more years of his bile and stupidity.

Now contrast that with how you will feel if instead you celebrate as a thoughtful, mature adult Democrat lays out a new program to help working people of all races and genders, and who promises to appoint progressives to the judiciary for eight years, who returns the nation to an aggressive stance combating climate change. I'm sure you want to do something to make this happen. Imagine you are not just doing this but leading it, and dozens of other volunteers in your neighborhood.

Reflecting on the Obama years, I believe we were successful in part because for those years the members of our team contributed not just the best work of our lives but were also our best selves. There is no professional feeling like that in the world, and it can be oh so fleeting. For five or six months this year, as a leader you have the opportunity to do your own best work and know that it counts, selflessly going to work with like-minded people to build a better future for your family and all our families.

At least twenty hours a week will be necessary for fulfilling your leadership obligations, so make sure you can make that work. If you can make it fit with all your other obligations, seize the moment. Raise your hand to be a local team leader. You'll work in partnership with the local field organizer from the candidate's national campaign and a few other leaders, covering a territory that could be large geographically or tiny, depending if it's rural or urban, and comprises a few hundred people, give or take, depending on the actual precinct numbers.

That staffer and you—from similar or if you're fortunate, very dissimilar backgrounds—will have each other's backs as you make history together and, quite likely, form a lifetime bond.

Let's get hypothetically specific. You live in Chippewa Falls, Wisconsin, population fourteen thousand, and our nominee's campaign has crunched the numbers and decided it needs 140 votes out of your precinct to add to the 1.6 million total votes they've predicted they need in order to win the Badger State.

This win number, as it is called, will reflect registration goals, as we have seen, and be based on the demographic composition of your precinct. How many new registered voters are required? (The registration "universe," in campaign lingo.) How many truly persuadable voters do you need to convert? (The persuasion universe.) Who are the sporadic voters in your precinct who will vote for the Democratic candidate if they vote at all? (The turnout universe.)

If you know Chippewa Falls well, you might even be

able to help supply some of that data. If not, you'll be more reliant on the campaign. Either way, this is how, in rough-and-ready terms, national campaigns work at the local level. This "universe" jargon may not be all that clear at first glance, but it gets superclear and real when applied to the precinct level. You need to register thirty new voters, work a persuasion universe of fifty, and cajole a universe of forty low-propensity voters to cast their ballots. Hey, it suddenly seems doable! You can deliver these votes.

You'll need help—and the help is all around you. You will start with names the campaign has from people in your precinct who have already signaled they want to help in the general election. You'll have volunteer leaders and volunteers from the nominee's campaign in the Wisconsin primary. You could well be one of them.

The local Democratic Party will have a list of reliable volunteers. Organizations like NextGen, SwingLeft, and your local union will also have names of people who have worked previously in local efforts and/or signaled their desire to get involved in the general election. The candidate's campaign will supply contact info on people in the Chippewa Falls precinct who have donated but not volunteered. These are hot leads, and it is up to you or your designated volunteer recruiter to call, text, or email the request that they sign up for volunteer shifts.

And/or what other tasks would they like to take on? Do they like to work in groups or alone with their computers? Everyone's got a role to play.

And of course, you'll reach out to your network—all the people you've been pestering to register, and your own social network—and build your own core volunteer cadre to supplement the campaign's lists, and work out from there.

It will be the campaign's responsibility, through your field organizer, to ensure that you and your crew have the facts and materials you need—most important, correct and actionable names in the registration and turnout and persuasion universes. What's "actionable" in this context? Real names of real people with real contact info and real data on where they stand in the election.

All this then becomes data that needs to be updated in real time as you gather new information: which issues most concern these specific voters; if new voters, will they perhaps need follow-up to support their commitment to turn out, and will they require help getting to the polls? Keeping those records up-to-date is a key job for a volunteer with basic computer skills.

The office should also supply brochures, window posters, yard signs, door hangers, e-cards for Instagram, whatever else you need to get the job done. If you think another tactic would work with a certain voter but you don't have what you need, ask for it. If they don't have it, find or make it yourself.

Your success—and the joy and satisfaction you get from leadership—will come in part from hitting your numbers in Chippewa Falls, which helps our nominee win Wisconsin, which in turn helps defeat Trump and wins the presidency. But I promise that you will also derive equal joy and satisfaction from the people you work with and meet—the human side of the effort.

You will become the face of the campaign in Chippewa Falls, even more so than the candidate. For this reason alone, you need to inspire people. Listen to them. Treat them well. Laugh with them. Understand that no two of us are alike, no two volunteers, no two voters. People may sign up to volunteer in the beginning because they are inspired by our candidate, and the stakes in this election are so high. But they will likely keep coming back, and perhaps working even harder than they imagined— because of you.

Now what about the 90 percent of you—give or take—who don't live in a battleground state? You will have a deep impact nonetheless, in large measure thanks to your social media networks, which don't recognize state lines and will penetrate deep into every state (the subject of chapter 2). The positive content you share on your social media platforms, and the pushback against the lies about immigration and health care you post, will penetrate deep into every state, including the battlegrounds, reaching swing voters and your compadres whom you have now persuaded to register and vote and have also armed sufficiently to become their own content distributors. You know the drill—but it's not a drill. It's the real world.

So if you live in Wheeling, West Virginia, or Fresno, California, or any of the other states that are probably settled affairs in the electoral college, you should feel that you are playing a helpful and constructive role in the states that are in play. Beyond the winning proposition that is social media, your financial contributions can fuel the campaigns in Wisconsin and Florida (more on that one shortly). And there are of course direct ways to engage in battleground state activity from beyond that state line.

Your ability to travel to battlegrounds to help out in the closing months and weeks will be dependent on a lot of factors. Do you live close enough to drive or hop on a bus that our nominee's campaign or a progressive organization is chartering to head across state lines? Can you find the time, given work and family schedules? If you have kids, can you arrange for child care or can you take them with you? It's a great experience for kids, especially if they are into the election. And when you are knocking on doors, you'll get a more interested and friendly reception if you are doing so with your ten- or twelve-year-old at your side.

If you live far enough away that you need to fly or take the train, can you afford the ticket or have the loyalty program points? What about lodging? Do you have friends or family in the area whom you can stay with? I hope that our nominee sets up a program that identifies supporters in battleground states who are willing to have out-of-state volunteers stay with them, defraying the need to pay for a hotel room. Of course this can also be a great way to make a new connection and share stories and motivations about your activism and the election. Only you can answer those questions, but I would suggest that if you have an interest in being in the middle of the action, begin working through those questions now and making a plan to make it work.

Out-of-state volunteers have a storied history in presidential politics. In 1960, John F. Kennedy's large family and supporters from Massachusetts fanned out to key primary states and then the battlegrounds in the general election, vouching for his character and leadership and answering voters' questions directly about their concerns with his age and Catholicism.

Bill Clinton famously employed the "Arkansas Travelers," a potent group of friends, family, and supporters to make the case for his candidacy in the primary states and general election, engaging in door-to-door and phone activity, generating helpful local press coverage in those key media markets about why folks from Arkansas felt so strongly about Clinton's candidacy that they would travel to New Hampshire and Ohio to spread the word.

George W. Bush had large contingents from the big state of Texas making the case for him in his historically close win over Al Gore in 2000, and helping to drive up Republican turnout in his tough reelection fight four years later.

In 2008, the Obama campaign used the power of the internet, on full display in presidential politics for the first time, to "scale" a focused effort highlighting the need for supporters to travel to battleground states, recruit volunteers, and/or do what they (or we) could to help with logistics and cost. Buses from the Bay Area of northern California rolled east to Reno, Nevada. Buses from Birmingham, Alabama, traveled down to northern Florida. We tried our best to make sure that when these amazing volunteers who traveled hundreds if not thousands of miles from home to Nevada or Florida or Virginia or Colorado, they were welcomed with open arms.

Maybe not wined and dined, exactly, but well taken

care of. They were expected, and the work they were asked to do was well-organized, smart, and meaningful. We felt so strongly about the value these long-haul travelers could provide our campaign that we pushed all those on our email list to consider signing up to travel. Tens of thousands did, some for a day, some for a month. It was amazing to watch the commitment and energy these amazing citizens brought to the effort.

One natural question you may have: How useful is it to have some stranger from Los Angeles engaging voters in exurban Wisconsin? Well, of course no two voters are exactly alike, and neither are two volunteers, so it's difficult to accurately predict how each conversation is going to go, but it can be quite effective with those Democratic voters who may not vote and others heavily negative on Trump who are considering the third-party option.

Let's say you and a friend have driven to Philadelphia from Syracuse, New York. You let the campaign know through an online sign-up form that you will be there for the third weekend in October. You are asked to show up at the campaign office on the north side of Philadelphia at ten a.m. on Saturday. You arrive on time and find yourselves in the company of dozens of other volunteers, both local and those from out of state.

The person in charge—maybe from the campaign, maybe a volunteer leader—explains that the focus for that day is to reach out by door and by phone to a universe of possible voters who the campaign believes are no risk to vote Trump, but a huge risk not to vote at all.

Maybe they've told a campaign volunteer directly that they're unsure about voting; or the campaign has not been able to confirm that they have pledged to vote; or they have registered for the first time so we have no voting history for them; or they are registered but have not voted in the last couple of elections; or they may have moved and therefore have a new polling location but probably don't know where it is.

You and your friend listen to the boss's introductory explanatory remarks and learn that you will be given a list of voters and a map. These could be downloaded on your phone with a walking route laid out just for you. Just follow the blue line. Here's hoping the best tech is fully operational during this cycle.

Let's say there are twenty voters. The campaign believes these are all voters who support our candidate, but you and your friend have to make sure they materialize in actual votes.

It's time to head out.

A good percentage of the doors you knock on will remain unopened. Of course it is a just a couple of weeks before a historically important election and almost everyone will know what you're up to and why you're ringing the doorbell.

But maybe they're not home, don't hear the door, pay no attention to politics, hate politics, aren't going to open the door for a couple of strangers if this visit is not preceded by a text from someone they know.

But eight people do open their doors. Eight out of twenty is a good haul. Through these conversations, you'll get a variety of critical data and have important conversations that you'll report on. The campaign will take in the new data, and take appropriate action to follow up.

Let's say four of the voters say they are definitely planning on voting. At your urging, they share their plan for when they will vote, where, and how they will get to the polls. Great. You can report on them as four votes that the campaign can believe are now in the bank.

Two of the voters are not sure if they are going to vote. The first voter says something like, "I hate Trump. But getting somebody new in there won't really change things. I'm busy and really don't have time for politicians. I doubt I'll vote."

This is your moment! You may decide to ask this potentially crucial voter what issues matter most, then explain our party's position on those issues, whether it's taxes or border security or anything else. You're prepared. You stress the differences between our candidate and Trump. You may say something as simple as, "If you hate Trump, do you really want to live through another four years of him?"

More quickly than you might believe in the beginning, you'll get a feeling for these conversations with your fellow citizens. You'll know whether it's best to go on the offense or the defense, or maybe someone just wants to talk about what's going on in their lives, about how this election will affect it. And you're prepared to talk with them for as long as it takes—this could be the most important conversation of your outing.

Let's assume that your engagement—whether on offense or defense—has an impact and this guy says, "I guess you're right. I'll do my best to vote. But I can't remember where I go to do it."

Pennsylvania has not enabled widespread early voting options, so most voters will need to show up at the polling place on Election Day. Boom! You just happen to have the polling location for this precinct right there in the canvassing app on your phone and written on your clipboard.

"You vote at George Washington Carver High School, down on W. Norris Street. Polls are open from 7 a.m. to 8 p.m."

"Thanks. I went there. You from around here, by the way? We just all call it Carver."

"Nope. I'm from Syracuse, upstate New York. Because New York is definitely going to vote for (ID our candidate, of course), I wanted to help somewhere where it's a jump ball. Pennsylvania is the main reason Trump is president. He won it last time. We have to make sure he doesn't win it again. I'll be thinking of you up in Syracuse on Election Day, hoping you can make it to the polls."

And of course you will leave this voter with a card with the polling location. That exchange has a very good chance of sticking. On Election Day maybe it's raining, traffic is bad coming home from work, this voter needs to run an unexpected errand for a family member, so it will not be our candidate who gets him to the polls. It will be you. He told that woman from—where was it? Syracuse—that he would vote, and he will.

Now let's say the other unsure voter conversation follows about the same script, though maybe you need to help her check if she reregistered after a job move. And you need to talk her through her disappointment after Clinton lost in 2016. That loss produced a lot of discouraged attitudes, and for some a sense that they don't recognize the country anymore, which means Trump will win again. You get her to a good place. She's voting.

The last two of the eight voters who do answer the door that Saturday afternoon are 100 percent sure they are voting, new information that you will capture and feed into the campaign's data blender. But you learn an even more important piece of information: both of these individuals are leaning toward a third-party candidate. The first thinks both major parties are corrupt, and she wants to send a message. The second's favorite candidate in the primaries lost, and now he can't get excited by our candidate—he disdains Trump, would never vote for him, but he's not excited by the Democrat.

It's your moment again! In both cases. Listen carefully to what these two critical Pennsylvania voters are saying, then use your heart and your head to determine the best approach. The one common denominator is they're not voting for Donald Trump. You may share some of your own concerns about our nominee as you learn more about their concerns. Such sharing leads to a more genuine and therefore effective conversation. Your core message to each of them: You don't like Trump, and there's only one way to get rid of him. Vote for the opposing major party candidate. Simple as that.

Let's say you have some success with voter number one. She says she'll think hard about swallowing her distaste for both major parties and vote for our nominee. The second voter remains steadfast in his refusal to vote for the Democratic candidate despite participating in the Democratic primary.

Both of these really important data points will now ascend into the cloud, and the campaign will deploy resources—advertising on the internet or through the mail and perhaps one or more person-to-person contacts with another volunteer, hoping to lock in voter number one and see if anything else can be done to unlock voter number two.

At the end of your shift, you can look back and count two voters who were disinclined to vote but now report they will. One leaning third-party voter may well be back in our column. Three voters in the whole big state of Pennsylvania in this whole big country of ours. How can that be worth the trip to Philadelphia from Syracuse?

Back to some simple math. Let's say on that Saturday 5,000 other canvassing volunteers in Pennsylvania recorded similar outcomes—an average of three voters in which our campaign could be more confident. That's 15,000 total. And the same results are reported on Sunday. We're at 30,000 for a weekend. And there are five weekends in October leading into 2020. That's a total of 150,000 voters we now feel more confident will be casting ballots to award Pennsylvania's must-win 18 electoral votes to our nominee.

Now, not all of these voters will follow through, and some were likely going to vote the right way anyway. But that universe of 150,000 voters is more than *three* times the margin Clinton lost Pennsylvania by in 2016. So yes, your trip from Syracuse was worth it. It was most definitely worth it.

If you believe fervently in beating Trump, and you have the time and means to travel to a battleground state, shame on you if you don't. That's a strong statement but a true one. You need to get fully into the fight.

On the other hand, you don't have to leave Syracuse to have a meaningful impact on the outcome of the election in the core battlegrounds.

Phone banking and texting into the same cohorts of voters in Philadelphia can result in acquiring the same data and intelligence, but locking in supporters of our nominee, that happens at the front doors.

Now, I'll be honest. There's no substitute for a person-to-person contact. I'd choose that over phone or text anytime. But it's certainly an important additive ingredient, and for sure there are voters who won't answer the door (or it's hard to get into their building). Digital contact, or even old-fashioned snail mail, is the only way to reach them.

You can help with the long-distance contacts from nonbattleground states in two ways.

Directly or in coordination with the DNC, our nominee will probably rent office space throughout the country for this very purpose: providing supporters who want to make a difference in the battlegrounds directly a place to gather to do so. The big cities will definitely have designated banks. Just Google "Nominee phone banking Seattle" or "Nominee campaign office Los Angeles" or go to our nominee's website, which should have an easy-to-navigate page for finding the local office nearest you. Farther afield, even a small local campaign office or the local headquarters of the Democratic Party will likely be set up with a phone bank. If that system is organized properly, you should be able to work with the same fresh lists of target names, based on real-time data, that are used for door-to-door canvassing.

The second option is to make the calls from your home using a list from the campaign, or attend or host a phone-banking get-together, with everyone on hand dialing into the same state, having a shared experience and a shared impact. Host one yourself. You know I think that's a great idea.

Don't get discouraged by hang-ups! Yes, you are telemarketing, but for a worthy cause, remember. You'll experience the same low-contact percentage of those canvassing on the streets—you'll find people not answering, whether cell or landline; not wanting to talk, saying they are busy; or being downright rude—but you will get through to some voters, and in every shift you work you will connect with a few people, and there will be enough others like you reaching out to target voters, day after day, month after month to yield a massive, positive, cumulative impact.

On the phone, you will have many of the same conversations you would have had at the front door. You will need to listen, most of all, but don't miss any opportunity to commune with these voters, try to gently persuade, impart important information about the voting process in the voters' state and precinct, whether this be early voting details in Florida, same-day voter registration in Wisconsin, or polling location details in Pennsylvania.

The campaign should also have some nonphone ways to help out in the battleground states. You may be given the option to write postcards to certain segments of voters, maybe new registrants in Detroit, congratulating them on becoming a first-time voter and assuring them how important their vote is to your family in Greenville, South Carolina.

You could be writing notes to voters in Miami who the campaign is convinced would support our nominee if only they'll actually turn out. You could write a very personal message about what this election means to you and your family, why you think their one vote in Florida could make all the difference. Florida should be the easiest venue for making this argument convincingly. I hate to sound like a broken record (if you remember vinyl) but if just 539 more Floridians had voted for Al Gore in Florida in 2000 . . .

I hope the campaign also adopts a program to allow supporters throughout the country to send notes to the precinct captains and neighborhood team leaders in battleground states, thanking them for their leadership on their behalf. Love a volunteer leader today!

A note from you in Boise, Idaho, to a volunteer leader in Elko, Nevada, saying you just wanted to thank them for all they are doing, you admire their commitment so much, all of the campaign's supporters throughout the country are rooting for them to succeed and win their area and their state for the Democrat. Such a note can get them to push through this tough day and give them motivation to have a better one tomorrow. It's hard work and they are doing it on behalf of all of us. They're the true heroes in the battleground states in this supremely important election.

MONEY

★ ★ ★

I f money is such a big deal in politics, why does it merit the smallest chapter in this book? Because my main point throughout is the supreme power of volunteers in a modern American presidential campaign. I want you to volunteer. This is how we'll win in 2020. Believe it or not, your time is more valuable to the campaign than your money.

Also, there are so many ways to lay out the big picture of volunteering to pique your interest and then show you all the ways you can join up. I hope you try many of them. Meanwhile, there's only one way to contribute money. Contribute money. Boring, though of course vitally necessary.

Finally, volunteering will be an amazingly fulfilling experience—and always challenging too because you are dealing with human beings, and human beings, well, they have issues. Getting the most out of any collection of men and women, building a culture of trust and honesty, and valuing empathy and selflessness? Extremely gratifying. Writing a check? Not as much, let's admit it.

Many people have asked me if their money is really needed, if their one-millionth of a billion-dollar nut will make a difference given the tsunami of money, billions and billions of dollars, now inundating the American electorate.

Well, think about your family. Is your financial contribution to the budget important? Yes. Incredibly so. Is it as important as your love? No. There's a rough analogy here, I think: yes, your one-millionth of a teaspoon counts; no, it's not as important as your time.

If you are thinking about making a sacrifice in order to make a contribution—perhaps forgoing a trip with an aging parent or putting off a car or appliance repair—please don't. Should we tragically lose in 2020, or win by too close for comfort, there will be a lot of reasons, but money will not be at the top of the list. There are enough financially secure people in this country to properly fund our campaign and make any financial sacrifice from you unnecessary. Prioritize your volunteer work, not your bank account. Devote as much time to the campaign as possible, helping us register, persuade, and turn out voters, while also recruiting other volunteers to do the same—and while always fitting this sacrifice around your family life and your work.

Of course it's easy for me to give priority to the volunteering because I know that the one campaign activity in the past most of you reading this book probably have in common is that you have already donated dollars to Democratic candidates, up and down the ballot. For those of you who did so in 2008 and 2012 to help elect and reelect Barack Obama, thank you, thank you, thank you. Your generosity helped us hire the staff, reach the voters, and communicate the message that secured two presidential victories. Many if not most of you have donated to one or more of the Democratic primary candidates in this election cycle, and you'll contribute to the winner pretty soon. My emphasis of the value of your time does not diminish the value of your money. If you can afford to give, we can't afford for you not to.

Why do you donate so generously? It's not for bragging rights, that's for sure. I do urge you to post news of a donation to your social media, explain your reasons, maybe spur others to follow suit. But the main reason we contribute is to send a message. Perhaps you were motivated by an answer to a tough question in a YouTube clip or in one of the gazillion debates. When we see and hear a candidate who speaks to us, the easiest way to register our approval is to whip out the phone and make an online donation. It feels good to put some teeth behind a positive reaction.

You may react in the same way to certain issues, controversies, and in this of all years, the latest outrage from the incumbent. During the "Muslim ban" travesty at the start of Trump's term, many Americans marched and went to airport protests, but the way most of us could register our horror at what was unfolding was to log on to the ACLU site and make a donation. Likewise, when Trump's accomplices instituted their vindictive policy of separating children from parents at the Texas border.

Most of us couldn't travel down there to help the heroic groups on the ground. The best way for us to fight back was to give money to local advocacy groups like RAICES (the Refugee and Immigrant Center for Education and Legal Services) and the Texas Civil Rights Project, who were doing all they could to stand up to our racist president's policies and help those affected. It most definitely could be that a tweet our sociopathic president sent out was so over the top and filled with so many lies that it motivated you to send another twenty-five dollars to the candidate you think has the best chance of ending the tweeting, at least from those under the imprimatur of the presidency. In any event, it feels like the best way to fight back.

And it *is* a great way to fight back. On these issues you probably can't send too many messages. Contributions really can unlock a ripple effect. If you let people know that you clicked and gave, many more will then follow suit.

Maybe your contributions to presidential campaigns have been spontaneous expressions of support. If so, you're an outlier. Most people don't volunteer their money, so to speak. One of the big problems with raising cash in a campaign is that it's so expensive. Maybe you supported another candidate in the primary but went straight to our nominee's website the day she or he clinched the nomination, and then you gave a donation. That's terrific—the candidate will need a donor base four or even five times as large as the one that sufficed for the primaries—but realistically most of this expansion will result from smart and persistent digital marketing that identifies, motivates, and secures financial support throughout the country.

In the end, our candidate should receive about five million individual donations, totaling close to a billion dollars. Many of these donors will also become volunteers directly through the campaign, a twofer.

There are still many donors who still respond best to mail solicitations (especially older donors). And such solicitations are not cheap. Fund-raising event costs, whether headlined by our candidate or a surrogate, add up. Dozens of events are held every week all around the country. Travel costs are a big-ticket item for our nominee, his or her spouse, and all the politicians, athletes, and celebrities whom we need on the ground in battleground states.

Legal costs, compliance costs, office rent for all the local offices throughout the country, insurance, and so forth. Thousands of staffers will be required to organize the work of the hundreds of thousands of volunteers, especially in the battleground states. If they can't afford them, the staff is spread too thin, our volunteer leaders are not properly supported, and the entire organization gets creaky, leaky, and less effective. The staffers are mostly young kids right out of college, and they're not making much for the sixteen-to-eighteen-hour days they are working, seven days a week, but it adds up fast, and all of it adds up even faster. The campaign is a large, complicated enterprise. It's a massive start-up.

Then there's the biggest of the big-ticket items: advertising and other forms of voter contact to reach all of our target cohorts. Television ads may run for five to six months in some major cities like Miami, Orlando, Philadelphia, and Phoenix, expensive markets. Radio ads. Mail pieces. Literature dropped at doors. I hope the largest segment of this category of spending will be for digital advertising on any and all platforms. The creation of all this content—film shoots, editing, video and print production—is very expensive. The market research and testing to determine the exact messages for these ads, and the targeting guidance behind the ad buys, is an almost-around-the-clock enterprise and on its own will cost millions.

The subject of the previous chapter—battleground states—and the subject of this chapter are synonymous, for all practical purposes. Follow the money and you'll know which states are the battlegrounds. Or from the campaign's perspective, determining the battlegrounds will determine where most of the money is invested. The campaign may throw some money at a few states just to test the waters; or to try to trick the opponent into matching an expenditure with its own expenditure.

These are not the big decisions. The most crucial decision of any presidential campaign is the identification of the real battlegrounds, where the real money is invested—the full-court press is composed of candidate time, surrogate time, staff, advertising, and the all-important registration and GOTV efforts. Those last two efforts are volunteer driven, but only the volunteers' time is free. Supporting it is cost intensive.

In short, the campaign has to ensure that the volunteers' time is carefully invested. Waste it and the election is lost.

A lot goes into the battleground decision. Let's take a quick look inside that sausage factory, where the first stop is the clear-eyed and cold-blooded assessment of whether the candidate can win a particular state. Do the various registration and turnout models look promising? Even if there is a credible path forward to compete in a close election in, say, ten states, this good news doesn't end the analysis. Can the candidate afford to win each of these states? Detailed budgets will be prepared throughout potential target states. Arizona will cost millions, North Carolina tens of millions, Florida upward of $50 million,

and Texas, should it truly become a possibility, Lord
knows how much the Lone Star State could cost, maybe
$75 million, maybe more. A mistaken judgment on Texas
could be fatal.

Are these resources really and truly on hand? No
fairy-tale dreaming allowed. Then do the math. Is the
appetite for states to target larger than the wallet? In all
likelihood, yes. Incredibly tough decisions follow, as the
computer software and the campaign leadership's instinct
and judgment mix and match combinations of states and
their costs. So many permutations. States like North Carolina and Arizona could have a strategic value above and
beyond the cold hard numbers. If we contest them, we
make the Trump campaign defend a wider swath of territory under the fear that their 26 combined electoral
votes become as winnable for the Democrats as the blue
wall's Wisconsin and Michigan, also 26 votes, guaranteed battlegrounds in 2020.

Taking a state off the electoral college chess board
due to a lack of resources is one of the toughest decisions
a campaign manager has to make, and it will be tougher
still if in the end, the lost electoral votes would have
made the difference between victory and defeat. Even
worse is to green-light a battleground state, only to realize a couple of months later that you really don't
have the resources to see it through. You've wasted mil-

lions, maybe more, and the optics are terrible. McCain pulling out of Michigan in 2008 is a good example of that terrible dynamic. Even for the Obama campaign in 2012, we sank a huge amount of resources into North Carolina, only to pull back on our spend in the closing weeks when it looked like it would be close but just out of reach.

The campaign will make its fund-raising and budget assumptions based on predictive modeling: number of donors now, how much their numbers will grow, and how much they will donate. The assumptions usually turn out to be quite accurate. Eerily so.

So you donors will have an enormous influence on the most important strategic decision the campaign makes—the target list for battleground states—especially if you give early in the cycle, when the big decisions are made.

As with volunteering, you must look at your financial contribution as a catalyst for others to act. As noted earlier, posting your donation on social media may spur others to do the same. But I repeat: do not sacrifice necessities for your family in order to contribute to this campaign. Just as there are more than enough people in the United States to defeat Trump if we can get them to the polls, there are more than enough people who can comfortably contribute and make sure money is not a reason we put ourselves at a disadvantage in the upcoming battleground wars.

So please give what you can if you can. And make it fun, and even meaningful along the way. I devoted an earlier chapter to the importance of hosting supporters and volunteers in all kinds of venues under all kinds of circumstances. You can make fund-raising a communal activity as well. This doesn't have to be an elaborate program. Pick a night and send out an email to everyone you know and suspect is a supporter of our nominee and/ or hates Trump.

Say something along the lines of, "I know many of you have already contributed to our candidate. I thought it would be nice to get together to thank those who have given, celebrate those who might this night, and coax the fence-sitters to join us so we can tell them how important their participation is. I'll have our candidate's best hits teed up on the TV, as well as some of Trump's worst. It will be a casual night, and folks are welcome to speak about why they have gotten involved, but it's really just a way for us to share our hopes, dreams, and fears for the election and strategize about how we can do more. And you can feel free to scream and shout about yesterday's presidential tweets. Because I promise you, there will have been something new to scream about."

It's that simple. Maybe have some snacks and drinks on hand, ask a few close friends to bring some as well. No fancy catering allowed. Have a sign-in table and a laptop or two as people enter. They can both contribute online as well as sign up for volunteer activities. If you want, ask a local elected official to come and say a few words, but that is by no means necessary. It's just a nice opportunity for people to gather and make their financial support more communal, and come to life, and perhaps encourage some new donors to give and some existing donors to give again. It would be a chance to process the election generally and the specific events of that week with others, laughing, sighing, chewing fingernails, whatever is appropriate for the moment.

If you can't host an event but are invited to one, please think hard about attending, even though it's not the kind of thing you usually do.

You could even do a lighter-touch method, asking all the people you think may be interested to give together, virtually. Maybe it would be after a particularly great day for our nominee that gets you pumped up, or a day where Trump reaches new depths of depravity, getting you pumped up in a less inspirational way. "OK, everyone, let's all make a donation in the next twenty minutes and post about it on Facebook. Let's tag each other and thank all those who do give in the comments. Let's try to get a hundred people to join us right now."

You know my theory: This election will be hard enough for us all to live through. It will be far easier to make it through together, on line and off.

7

THE CAMPAIGN

★ ★ ★

As a citizen determined to deny Donald Trump a second term and thereby strengthen, if not actually save, our democracy, much of your impact in this election season will be accomplished on your own time, not through any formal channels. Not waiting to be asked, you'll be asking the question, "What more can I do?"

Whether it's engaging in one-on-one conversation with a friend or a cousin or a coworker who's wrestling with the decision, working your own network to register and volunteer, engaging in debate and sharing persuasive content on social media, and/or donating money, your daily advocacy is irreplaceable.

And at some point—hopefully the day our nominee is clear—you will also work with and through the candidate's official campaign. This is the operation that has prepared the literature and set up the phone banks and created the contact lists and linked everything to the GPS interface for the canvassing teams. The interface between you volunteers and the campaign apparatus is so crucial, it's the subject of this chapter.

We know what the volunteers do for the campaign—nothing less than deliver the margin of victory, that is, the registrations, the canvassing, the recanvassing, the re-re-canvassing; if necessary, the rides to the polls, the actual votes. Now I want to consider what the campaign can and should do for you. The more you know, the better you'll be able to evaluate what it is doing, and how you can help make everything easier and more effective. No matter how much of a sacrifice your personal work is, no matter how far you have come in order to help, no matter if you're working in your hometown or a thousand miles away, it is essential that the campaign staff honor your time and commitment with the tools, data, materials, and culture to make it both a rewarding and effective experience.

I want this chapter to be useful for both volunteers and the campaign's professional staff.

I started my career as a canvasser and organizer, and nothing I've learned has changed my own innate belief in the power of people to do their best and achieve great goals if the support staff and leaders give them their best too. The influence moves both ways. As a former community organizer, Barack Obama had reached this same conclusion, so he insisted that those who wanted to join our cause in 2008 were respected and valued. As did Michelle Obama.

In 2008, in both the primary contest against Hillary Clinton, with Obama the decided underdog, and in the general election against John McCain, a toss-up from the get-go, our campaign's commitment to nourishing our grassroots volunteers was essential—indeed, it was *the* essential ingredient in victory.

We had put the volunteers first, and nothing changed for the 2012 reelection campaign. I don't believe any presidential campaign in living memory has given more consideration to the experience of our volunteers. If our candidate called me from the road, or if I was traveling with him and he pulled me aside after an event, it was almost always about the same question. Not debates, not ads, not campaign strategy. He would be advising me that a volunteer or a local field organizer on our staff had told him they weren't getting everything they needed. Maybe the data and lists were screwy lately, or there was not enough literature on hand, or not enough yard signs.

I might have said something like, "But boss, yard signs don't vote." This expression originated who knows where, but every campaign manager is tempted to invoke it as a way to save money with the nickel-and-dime stuff. My boss would invariably say, "So you're telling me that with all the money we're raising from the very people who are working so hard for us, we can't make sure they get enough lousy signs to show their support? Especially for a candidate who might be a Republican, and whose yard sign will send a message?"

And the signs would be shipped right away. For Barack Obama, the volunteers were how he charted his course. If we weren't serving them first and foremost, we probably weren't doing anything else as well as we could. Our Iowa caucus campaign team—this was in the very early days of 2007, about twenty months prior to the general election—decided to memorialize their approach by painting the words *Respect, Empower, Include* on our headquarters in Des Moines and subsequently in the dozens more local campaign offices we opened up throughout the Hawkeye State.

From Paul Tewes, our Iowa state director, on down . . .

actually there was no "down." The staff lived their inclusive motto every day. So did the precinct captains. So did all the volunteers who had been there from the beginning, as they welcomed those who joined up later. The Iowa kids were the most talented, selfless, driven crew I've ever been around. With all of them, there was a stirring belief in Barack Obama; in the need to turn the page from the Bush years; in the desire to make progress on issues from health care to climate change. The sum of their efforts became greater than the parts. Every Iowan who walked through our campaign office doors was treated as if he or she were the most special person in the world. Because it was true. It wasn't manufactured. It was magical. And the caucus results reflected as much: Obama, 38 percent (more than twice what we'd started out with a year earlier); Hillary Clinton and John Edwards, 30 percent apiece, with Edwards a nose ahead of her.

In 2020, I don't know whether our nominee will motivate people to the same degree Barack Obama did. But I do know our candidate had better insist that the staff treats everyone as if they are the most special people in the world too. Let's hope this comes easily and naturally. Putting volunteers first—"Respect, Empower, and Include" or the equivalent—must be baked into the campaign DNA. It cannot be faked. And much of the motivation needs to come from the ground up—staffers pushing and pulling one another, congratulating and lifting up those establishing the right culture in their region and pointing out those who are falling short. It needs to be as easy and intuitive as anything in life so that you don't even think about it. You just do it.

Logically, you volunteers are the first and most important customers of the campaign, coming before even the voters, because you are the connective tissue with the voters.

We can debate Amazon's business model, but I hope our nominee's campaign has the high level of consistent, excellent customer service as Amazon's does. The few times I've had problems with Amazon, the interactions actually left me more impressed. They move fast, they rectify mistakes, and they trust their customers. It's in the DNA of the company.

It doesn't take long for any retail customer to get a reading on an unfamiliar store. Likewise, with you as a potential volunteer with the presidential campaign. You'll know this outfit's attitude toward you as soon as you begin the first interaction, in person, on the phone, or online. If it's not genuinely welcoming, don't hesitate to let them know directly, or even post your reaction or complaint on social media.

No one getting back to you? Not being prepared for

the number of volunteers who showed up for a shift? General disorganization in the local field office?

Think about the snafu and suggest and help them change what needs to be changed. There is too much at stake to be shy about this. If they get this wrong with the volunteers, aren't they likely to get it wrong with voters? I'm afraid so. And they will probably need your help fixing other stuff that's wrong. From making sure there is enough water on hot canvassing days to making sure the office is decorated and organized in a way that is both inspiring and efficient.

I hope the campaign spends a lot of time in dialogue with volunteers, formally and informally, to understand what will be the most helpful and effective way for the office to help the volunteers do the work they want and need and are desperate to do in order to help elect a different president. In the private sector, they call this *user research*: really understanding at a fundamental and deep level how the customers are living their lives, how the organization or company fits into these lives and aspirations, and then how to generate the best experience and therefore loyalty.

Campaigns do the same thing regarding key voter segments. Too often, though, they don't apply the same rigor to understanding their volunteers, learning more about their motivation, what drives them to want to be involved, what would make it a better and more effective experience for them.

The good news: the basic user research regarding the first customers for the Democratic presidential campaign is pretty clear—I'm sure you hear the same things I do. What do you volunteers want? You want to help save the country you love from further damage and embarrassment by expelling the incumbent. You want to work hard in that cause, you want an up-to-date tech campaign, and you don't want your time and energy to be taken lightly, much less wasted. And given the stakes this year, you don't think all this is asking too much.

Here are some clear requirements for making your volunteers' experience as effective as possible. The list is anything but definitive, but let's begin with the most effective ways to play offense, sharing positive content with a voter with doubts, and defense, fighting back against all the lies and smears. This is one critical set of tools the campaign must nail right now. By the time you're reading this book (Spring 2020), I hope our eventual nominee has this in their pipeline. It's getting late.

In this digital war, speed is of the essence. Above all,

your response must be lightning fast. You see something ridiculous on Facebook or in an email chain, and you want to push back against it. You have a matter of seconds, literally, to find the responsive and persuasive content you need and copy and share it easily, and then move on with your day.

You can always start with Googling or searching on YouTube or looking around the room for potential help. But the best way to accomplish this would be a simple app whose only function is sharing content for our distributed rapid-response army. There's a way to create an easy, all-in-one interface, organized by issue (immigration, taxes, health care, education) and by medium (infographic, article, video, photo). For playing defense, the equivalent on this app would be an up-to-the-moment catalogue of all the latest lies, smears, and presidential insults that are flying across your phone and computer screen, along with the oldies but goodies. This would be a modern-day version of the Obama Fight the Smears website from 2008, updated for the smartphone era of politics.

This isn't just a cool-sounding kind of idea I think is good to include in the book. It's a dead-serious requirement for any modern campaign.

Does our candidate's campaign already have such an interface? If so—and I hope so—make sure every volunteer can access it instantly on their smartphone or tablet. If the campaign doesn't have this collated rapid-response rebuttal app for playing both offense and defense, can you make one? Some of you volunteers will be designers and engineers, and probably have better computer skills than the campaign pros. Use those skills. Come up with a prototype. See a need, jump in and fill the breach and help win the election.

The campaign must also have a version of this function on its website, easy to find and use, for those who prefer engaging in these knife fights on a laptop or desktop. And all other organizations that are engaged in the battle to defeat Trump—from NextGen to the Service Employees International Union (SEIU) to Planned Parenthood to the Sierra Club—should have similar tools on the specific issues their members care most about and will want to be most voluble on, offensively and defensively. Make sure everyone knows what all the links are.

You will need a printed cheat sheet that you can carry with you when canvassing, so you can look things up on the spot and inform your folks behind the front doors of the best links. Someone—or a small group—needs to be responsible for updating this material in almost real time. What could be more impressive to a voter than an instant source of information or rebuttal to some silly Republican attack that happened early this morning? A fast, efficient communications operation in the campaign may imply a fast, efficient communications operation in the new administration taking over in 2021. Man, you guys are on the ball! A may-vote citizen and/or a may-vote-for-a-third-party citizen might make that connection. Give them a reason to.

When supporters have an urge to share a good idea or good content with their social media network, or to respond to yet another falsehood, ten seconds is the longest it should take for them to do this. If it takes longer, many people will give up, and an opportunity is lost.

Ten seconds, you say? That's a crazy standard to be held to. No, if anything, it's too long. People are used to getting what they want, the answers they need, the content they've heard about instantaneously—two to three seconds. And that's the population as a whole, including senior citizens.

The younger the age cohort we are talking about, the higher the bar for lightning-fast speed. Remember the recent industry study trying to understand why millennial consumption of breakfast cereals was dropping precipitously? The number one reason wasn't nutrition, cost, or taste. The number one reason was that eating breakfast cereal takes too long to clean up. Think about that. For my generation, Gen X, ease was the appeal. Shake it out of the box, add milk, eat, put bowl in sink, rinse bowl. But for a younger millennial, picking up food at Dunkin or a bodega is far preferable to the apparently complex and time-consuming process of eating a meal out of a box.

And Generation Z? Forget about it. Standing in a line even four deep is too inefficient for many of them. They're going to order ahead so their mobile order is ready at the counter—warm, paid for, and disposable. A busy Starbucks or Peet's Coffee has more than one designated employee working the mobile ordering line to keep things moving in the morning.

I go on at some length about this speed thing because I'm convinced it's very important. The tools we all need to make the case for our candidate must above all else be as easy and fast to use as picking up your latte, ordering the Uber, shopping on Amazon, or booking a room or home on Airbnb. People who are busy helping out the campaign between all the other pieces of their lives will not expect—or accept—a jankier experience or interaction with our nominee's website and apps than they get from the commercial sites they visit all day, every day. If you are finding that, don't be shy about pointing it out, and better yet, suggesting ideas for improvement. We won't win this election by ignoring areas for improvement that are hiding in plain sight.

It's clear by now that I hope you will be charging ahead on your own—don't wait for the campaign—making the positive case, putting out the substantive arguments for our candidate and against Trump, punching back against the lies and Infowars crazy-town stuff with your own rebuttals. Of course this will be incredibly effective. But not everyone will have the time, the desire, or the confidence to do so. Their needs must be addressed. Here's an idea: make it your job to circulate a weekly list of new links, new articles, and new arguments within your volunteer circle. Then they can follow suit.

So the first requirement: *speed*. The next requirement: *accuracy*.

I'm speaking now primarily about the various kinds of data and lists the campaign asks you to work with. All of it must be up-to-date and ready for action. Whether you are working from home, downloading a list of names and numbers of registration targets you are going to call in Florida; or have traveled to Michigan to knock on doors to get out the vote; or are sitting in a phone bank in Biloxi on Election Day, dialing registered voters in Philadelphia who have not yet voted—you want all that information, usually provided by the campaign, to be as deadly accurate as possible. We can't expect perfection—voters change their minds, and there can be data-entry errors—but perfection should be the aspiration.

If you are calling a citizen and asking her to register to vote in Miami—and she registered two weeks ago, that's a waste of your time, her time, and the campaign's resources. If you are canvassing in Grand Rapids, Michigan, in October and two consecutive voters say they are voting for our nominee—and they told someone else from the campaign last week—it's another waste of everyone's time, and you may ultimately not have much of it to knock on the doors of two voters farther down the list who really are undecided. And we may have tested the patience of those two voters. Man, you guys are dropping the ball! This is not what we want them to be thinking.

If you call a voter in West Philadelphia on Election Day, start your pitch, and he says with annoyance, "You're the second person who's called. I voted at 8:30 am this morning!," all you can do is thank him profusely, but it's still a waste of time on both ends. But he did vote, so what's the harm? Well, you made that call instead of another one, and it's a likely sign that the lists, farmed out to people throughout the country from West Philly, have other errors in them too.

Nothing is more dispiriting for everyone—campaign staffers and volunteers—than when a group of canvassers returns to the local field office exhausted after hours out knocking doors—that's good—but also annoyed because the voter data was inaccurate. It's hard enough to find your time to donate in the first place. If you feel it was then a waste of time—you were talking to the wrong voters about the wrong issues and no one pays attention to what you have learned when you return to headquarters—it's fair to expect that you may not come back.

The campaign should view its voter data first and foremost through how it will affect the experience their hardworking volunteers are going to have. Sending a GOTV mailer piece to a voter who already voted early, or delivering a "persuasion ad" on health care (an ad directed at someone who still needs persuasion) to a voter who wears a MAGA cap is a waste of some money. But what is far more precious is your time. The campaign simply can't trade in incorrect and out-of-date information.

This standard must also apply to all the independent groups doing critical voter contact as well. Whether it's Indivisible, NARAL, UFCW, or the Association of Flight Attendants, you don't want your own members or those volunteering with your organization engaging voters based on dated information. There are technical fixes for all these problems, and you will have workers who can implement them, but you have to know about these problems in the first place. You need good feedback from your members. In fact, encourage it. Tell your volunteers you don't just invite but welcome examples of bad data.

All of these groups should be working together to pool their data and update the information collectively and in real time. Sounds utopian, I know, but it's totally feasible technically. We have these resources. Everyone wants to send Donald Trump packing, so let's get it done.

So we have the fast and accurate requirements for information, and I would add to that a third one: it also needs to be as detailed as possible.

Let's say our canvasser in Grand Rapids talks to a voter on the "undecided" list who truly is undecided and persuadable. She tells our canvasser she has not made up her mind. She's wrestling with Trump's character, and his tax cuts just made the rich richer, she knows this, but she's also concerned our nominee will be bad for the small business where she works.

We hope our canvasser is prepared with an effective pitch about all the ways our candidate will help small businesses; we hope the canvasser seals the deal, but that's hard sometimes. Maybe the canvasser is not all that prepared on the issue. Either way, the next step is critical: the canvasser needs to capture the details of the exchange and feed them into the voter database as explanatory notes. Back at the office, someone will key in this feedback and that voter will start seeing ads about our candidate's plan to help small business in her mailbox and on her phone.

But you, the volunteer, can also zero in on this voter. Get into her hands more information on what seems to be her key concern. Who should do this? Your friend who runs a small business sounds like a good idea. Have her write a note or send an email to personally address the issue from the small-business owner's perspective.

This mechanism for following up should be SOP, but it won't happen without the richness of those explanatory notes. It's tragic if we lose this voter because no one takes the time or has the technical means to put on the electronic record the incredibly valuable and specific information about this torn battleground voter, so the campaign never finds out what would get her off the fence and into our corral.

How do the volunteers access the voter data? Through the electronic tools provided by either the campaign or one of the progressive organizations. By definition, just about, the tools delivering it are as important as the data. In the old days we used mimeograph machines, stuffed envelopes, and dialed phones. Ideal today—mandatory, I'd say—is a single app that works seamlessly on the smartphone, tablet, laptop, or big-screen office computer. It can be used by anyone authorized to interact with voters on behalf of the candidates. Download a list of target voters onto your phone when you've created a free hour in your life. When you auto dial a given voter, the correct script to use pops up on the screen. Maybe your exchange concerns registration, or follow-up on an issue involving the voter (he's thinking third party), or follow-up concerning a key issue of concern reported by a canvasser three days ago (the "small businesses" voter) issue. Whatever it is, the app has a one-stop link for recording the important and relevant information from the conversation, which is then fed back into the campaign's servers.

Tools, data, and support should be at your fingertips when you are canvassing. If Waze can direct you through traffic jams in Los Angeles and El Paso, surely our candidate's campaign can provide equally accurate technology that directs canvassers on a walking route, hitting the target doors, skipping the others, feeding you the pertinent information about this house call as you walk up the sidewalk, then recording your results instantaneously and easily as you walk back down the sidewalk. What a huge leap in efficiency and accuracy from the old ways—a significant motivation for the digital natives to return again and again.

I know—some volunteers will want to work with a

more traditionally analog interface, making their phone calls from paper lists or from names and numbers on their laptops, or canvassing off printed maps and with paper voter lists. This will be less efficient on the back end, but that's okay. I hope our nominee enables volunteers in this way too. This election will likely be incredibly close. Can the campaign afford to turn away anyone's offer of help? No. It should supply them with whatever material they feel comfortable with. Plus, a printed map never crashes or runs out of battery life! We have to meet volunteers—young or old, hip or vintage—where they are, just as we seek to do with important voter groups.

Only a firm and unshakable commitment to funding the field operation will pull this off. Which may seem obvious, but the campaign's commitment to you, the volunteer, will be tested from day one. There is always pressure from HQ to underfund the grass roots in order to feed the media budget. This is true in just about every campaign, large and small.

But the decision about funding the airwaves or the ground game is a decidedly false choice, just as the choice between focusing on "persuasion" voter targets or turning out the vote in the Democratic base is also false. Set your goals, then allocate your resources, not the other way around—that's the better approach, for both political campaigns and businesses. A business wants new customers, wants to retain old customers, wants to disrupt itself (R&D), wants a stable workforce, wants to make money. Based on these basic elements, funding choices have to be made, and those choices reflect the company's highest priorities at any given time. Amazon, Facebook, Airbnb, and many other internet start-ups famously put the emphasis on bringing in new customers. Thanks to venture capital, they didn't need to worry about actually making money. That could come later. Sometimes, much later.

A political campaign does not have the luxury of playing that long game, calibrating and adjusting all the angles over many years. It has a very short time period in which to maximize performance and win an election. In the discussion of the battleground states, I took us into the sausage factory to see how campaigns make the crucial decisions, how the "win numbers" are developed, how resources will be allocated among the various expense categories. One of those categories is the volunteers' grassroots ground game. The budget for each potential battleground is unique, and the percentage allocation formula for all states won't work because expenses vary by category from state to state. Obvious example: overhead costs and media buys will all cost more in Florida than in Michigan.

After that background, this point: far too many campaigns want to think the grassroots work, the campaign's field operation, can be done on the cheap. Even a well-funded campaign, even a well-funded *presidential* campaign will often try cannibalizing the field operation money in order to beef up the advertising budget to reach swing voters. This campaign may hire fewer paid campaign field organizers than they originally planned, meaning each organizer is responsible for a greater area as measured by geography and voters. This would mean that you, a volunteer leader, will have less access to your organizer partner, whose attention and workload may be spread too thin, making your job harder and making it more difficult for the campaign to reach its organizational goals in your area.

Skimping on the budget may mean the campaign will pay to open fewer offices. Fewer everything—yard signs, literature, pizza. You name it. Everything gets squeezed. Potential volunteers will have to travel a longer distance to reach a local field office, providing a disincentive to volunteer at all. Fewer volunteers means fewer voter contacts, which means you may end up with fewer new registrants, fewer persuadable voters converted at the doors and on the phones, and ultimately, fewer voters who turn out on Election Day.

To me, what's crazy about this skimping—and should be frustrating to you should it happen in your locale—is that the decision to skimp does not result from a debate about the number of votes the grassroots field operation needs to produce to get to the win numbers in the state, the region, the precinct. That's settled. No, the decision comes all too often from a belief the one element the campaign can risk starving is the ground game. The belief rests partly on the fact that it's hard to measure what your opponent is spending on the ground. Meanwhile, both sides' expenditures on TV, radio, and digital are public. If the campaign is being outspent in those mediums, especially if it's getting outspent heavily, or if it believes that turning the tables and outspending the opponent on the media front will gain a decisive advantage, it becomes incredibly hard to maintain discipline and stick to the original plan, keeping the grassroots funding wholly in place. Great will be the temptation to buy one more ad rather than support one more volunteer, to spend more on screens, less on screen doors.

We call that robbing Peter to pay Paul. Perhaps the ads do gin up some additional "persuasion" targets who may pay dividends on Election Day, no guarantees, but likely more votes are lost by not having the resources in place to execute the registration and turnout strategy fully.

Such was the situation for Team Obama in 2012, when unlike in the 2008 race against John McCain, we were getting badly outspent by the Romney campaign over the summer as Romney exited the primaries and built out for the general. Don't get me wrong. Thanks to the generosity of our donors, we were raising funds effectively, and at the end of the campaign would reach our finance goals, but sometimes you just get outspent no matter how well you do. The culprit was mainly the "outside game," those supposedly independent efforts supporting the candidates. The Republican super PACs were flooding the airwaves and computers with negative ads, while our equivalent outside resources were anemic and not closing the gap. Many Democratic donors—understandably but frustratingly, in my view—had and still do have a revulsion toward funding super PACs. They consider it too "dirty," a game played by Karl Rove, Sheldon Adelson, and the Koch brothers, not by clean and pristine progressive donors.

There was no magic $100 million sitting around to solve our problem that summer. In some markets, including Orlando and Des Moines, we were getting outspent two to one, which made a lot of us more than just a little uncomfortable.

Our staff and consultants on the creative and paid media side of the house were treating this as a DEFCON 1 alert. In the absence of the magic pot of gold, or even just a plain vanilla surplus, they demanded that we raid the field budget so we could survive the advertising onslaught. This painful situation created one of the most important calls of the campaign, and the one I'm probably proudest of.

It was the first Saturday in September and I was in Iowa with President Obama, who was speaking on a farm in Dallas County, surrounded by hay bales. I hopped on a conference call with Jim Messina, our campaign manager in 2012, and David Axelrod, my partner in crime and our senior strategist. We had to make a decision—do we stay the course, or do we cut back the field budget, especially in expensive states like Florida, Ohio, and Virginia?

It's no fun getting outspent by your competition in marketing and advertising dollars, whether you are marketing a candidate or a car service or a face cream. You know your opponents are reaching people critical to your success with more messages, and you have to assume, smart messages. It hurts. But for Messina, Axelrod, and me, it came down to two things—the numbers and our Obama campaign four years earlier. In Florida, as explained earlier, registering tens of thousands of voters in Miami-Dade County was critical to having any prayer of winning the state. In exurban and suburban Ohio, we had to have door-to-door, neighbor-to-neighbor, almost-around-the-clock contact with persuadable voters. In the Hampton Roads area of Virginia, we needed the ultimate turnout to ensure a win there. And we knew from

2008 that none of this would happen if we didn't believe in the power of the grass roots—and not just belief but backup for that belief by funding it fully. So we decided to accept getting outspent in media, at least for that period, and take our chances with our volunteer troops on the ground.

After Obama finished speaking and shaking hands and doling out hugs and high fives to the Iowans in attendance, he made his way to "the Beast," as the presidential limo is called by the Secret Service. We were on our way to . . . somewhere. The roadshow becomes a blur. I had walked over to the limo, anticipating his arrival, but was still on the call. He saw me on the phone, pacing around and looking intense, as he shook the last few hands of the local volunteers who had helped out at this event. I was pretty much always on the phone, but when I finally jumped in beside him, he asked sardonically, "Were you dealing with a real problem or talking Philly sports with someone?"

Obama did not have much interest in the minutiae of campaign budgeting decisions, but given what I thought was the import of our situations and the decision we had to make, I filled him in.

He asked, "How long was your call?"

"About forty-five minutes."

"Well, that's about forty-four minutes longer than it

had to be. We're here because of the grass roots and will be reelected because of the grass roots, so don't mess with that."

In retrospect, it really was that simple, I guess. We had gotten all tangled up in analyzing or second-guessing other people's strategies, and had lost sight of our own North Star for almost three-quarters of an hour. That clarity of mission and purpose is what we need this time. All of us will need it, most importantly the candidate who proclaims the sanctity of funding the grassroots operation, the campaign team who receives it loud and clear and then provides to everyone in the trenches everything you will need to be successful, whether you are an infrequent volunteer or a precinct leader.

If you are asked to volunteer, asked to give your time and talents, and constantly assured how important it is, the campaign must then honor and respect your commitment by making sure the grassroots campaign is resourced fully and effectively, even when it's tempting to cut some budgeting corners.

Many campaigns will ask for money, promising it will help pay for field organizers or local offices or supplies for local volunteers. If you are one of those contributors or fund-raising targets, and you see the grassroots efforts undernourished, give, yes, but also lift your voice. Point it out, even complain.

If you, a veteran precinct captain in Wisconsin, tweet at the nominee that your team is working hard but with fewer resources than you need, fewer than you had in the Obama campaigns, I promise your warning will get the attention and discussion it deserves.

We have an election to win: one of the most important in our country's history. A lot that has affected the race has already happened and much more will continue to happen that is beyond our power to control. The state of the economy. Pandemics. Mass attacks, foreign or homegrown. Tensions or outright conflict or war. The quality of the campaign Trump musters.

But there is a great deal of importance that we can control—we, the volunteers and the official campaign apparatus. The volunteers can control our commitment, our effort, our enthusiastic and infectious joy in the endeavor. The campaign can control the quality of the tools and data and TLC they bring to the party. Let's hope they also bring some serious joy to this serious task— anything hard is easier when it's fun too.

8

VOTING

★ ★ ★

In the 2020 presidential election, the Democratic nominee will enjoy more support among the roughly 250 million eligible voters than will Donald Trump. I would hazard a guess that the number is likely close to 55 percent. Perhaps a bit higher. Among those actually registered, the support levels slip a bit, but the good news is our nominee will enjoy a clear majority of support among the 175 million registered voters.

Big advantage for the Democrat, no matter who it is. Demographic modeling, polling, and voting history patterns tell us all this. Add the new registrants we need to add before Election Day, and our advantage swells.

However, actual election results over many campaigns prove that Republicans are "higher propensity voters," in the lingo. They get to the polls and vote more consistently than Democrats, without much prodding. We can match them, but it takes a lot of time, work, and money.

In 2016, registered Democrats voted at lower rates than registered Republicans, alarmingly so when you look at younger minority voters. And white voters who did not go to college, a Trump base, saw their percentage of the electorate surge over 2012 levels.

If we have to deal with the same discrepancy in 2020, big advantage Trump.

But the respective advantages balance out, right? I'm afraid not. Without any effort at all, Donald Trump starts with an advantage in terms of support levels materializing into actual votes. Add the fact that there are more conservatives than liberals in traditional battleground states, and that advantage gets even greater.

Trump starts closer to the goal line than we do.

The solution for Democrats? I'll quote one of the best campaigners in American history: "Organize the whole state, so that every Whig can be brought to the polls . . . divide the county into small districts and appoint in each a sub-committee . . . make a perfect list of voters and ascertain with certainty for whom they will vote . . . and on election day see that every Whig is brought to the polls."

That campaigner was Abraham Lincoln. The year was 1840, when he was a member of the Illinois legislature.

Almost 180 years later, such a "perfect list" is the aspiration of all political campaigns, large and small. By decree of the numbers, we must work harder in 2020 to make certain our lists are as close to perfect as possible. Do everything possible to ensure that we are talking to the right voters about the right things at the right time. This is the only way we can win. Otherwise, all the work, money, inspiration, perspiration, rallies, debates, ads, posts, laughs, and tears will come to naught.

GOTV is the acronym for Get out the Vote, which is the mother of all bottom lines. When I first started in politics, our tactics on this vital front were much less precisely targeted than they are today. We made large assumptions based on larger demographic and geographic assessments about the county, district, or state. There was very little individual data, and what we had was crude, maybe a list of voters we had talked to at some point in the campaign, identified as supporters, and intended to contact a second time near Election Day. So not too long ago, certainly through the 1990s, GOTV consisted of sending mail, telephoning, and knocking on the door of everyone in a high-performing Democratic precinct—a college community, say, or an urban center— and encouraging each and every one of them to vote.

Of course we knew that even the strongest Democratic precinct is, say, 85 percent or even 90 percent loyal, still leaving a chunk of vote for the Republican regardless of who calls them or shows up at the front door. I remember asking about this little problem in the first general election campaign I worked on, for Senator Tom Harkin of Iowa in 1990. If we contact all the registered voters in those strong precincts, aren't we worried we'll be turning out supporters of our opponent too?

Yes, came the answer, but it's the price we pay for making sure we drive as many of your own supporters out to the polls as possible. Think about the inefficiency. Volunteers were out there working hard to get out the vote among supporters who, in many cases, didn't need the reminder and at the same time encouraging supporters of the opponent to vote. Such were the limitations of the data and technology back in the day. Today we have the computer-based ability to take into account consumer and behavioral data and make detailed person-by-person and house-by-house distinctions to find the needle who may behave electorally different from the haystack.

Now, I understand that with many people concerned about online privacy—unwanted, unwarranted, and unauthorized tracking, and demographic profiling of all kinds—these tactics in a political campaign may sound a little creepy. But it's going to happen across all aspects of our life. I am a pragmatist, and given the stakes are we going to disarm?

Because they surely won't.

It's essential to spend the extra time, care, and resources on those voters we believe are more likely to support us but are also more likely to slip away and not vote at all. Smart, tech-savvy targeting is vitally necessary. If we're interested in winning this year, or any year in the future, it's how we have to compete. Fact of life.

Everyone's voting history is accessible to campaigns: when you voted and where, though of course not for whom. Campaigns try to focus on voters who could be at risk of not turning out, which is usually defined as someone who has missed voting in some elections, whether they be state, local, or federal. I'd also focus on all new registrants, who have no voting history.

Ideally, the campaign and its volunteers will have talked to as many individual voters as possible so that in addition to the demographic documentation, we have original, personalized data and information to inform our decisions about how to treat a specific voter. Definitely a supporter? If not, what's the problem? Definitely going to vote? If not, what's the problem? Voting early or by mail? I hope it's clear by now in this little treatise that no information is more accurate and valuable than that gleaned from direct person-to-person contact.

The campaign puts into the blender as much data as possible: each voter's past voting history, gender, race (when that can be identified), consumer information (income, car type, likely TV viewing habits, internet habits, news consumption), census information, polling, surveys, and any information gathered by personal interaction a volunteer on the campaign may have had—the most important kernel of them all.

And out pop the scores—one for "support," one for "turnout." Definitely voting for the Democrat? Your support score is 100. Always wearing a MAGA cap? That earns a 0. Legitimately undecided? You're a 50.

Regarding turnout, scoring 100 means you're a lock to vote. The lower that number drops, the better the chance that you will not, push comes to shove, get to the polls, much less vote early.

These numbers are used to determine what further actions are required by the campaign's volunteers to ensure your specific vote. You score 100 on support and 100 for turnout? Nothing to worry about there, and I hope the campaign leaves you alone. You score 50 and 50? If you don't hear from at least one volunteer, something is very, very wrong in the ground campaign.

The value of those numbers doesn't end there. They are also used to build "look alike" audiences (which is also how most consumer companies use platforms like Facebook to advertise and reach potential customers). The software puts together voter cohorts of people with scores close to yours. So even though the campaign volunteers will not have talked to all these voters—in fact, it will have talked with only a sample despite all the best efforts—the models' support and turnout numbers will predict which way every single voter in America will go on November 3.

Of course the models won't be 100 percent right, but they were eerily accurate in 2012, with President Obama's reelection campaign. We did have the advantage of being the incumbent. We had a very good sense of the electorate as it related to Barack Obama. We had a lot of good data about voter opinions over a five-year period. And Mitt Romney was a much more traditional Republican nominee than Trump, so it was easier to model his support and turnout scenarios. And the third-party vote was much smaller than in 2016. In the end, we had some states in which our win margin was within .10 percent of the prediction. Some of our estimates of the early vote breakdown in states like Ohio were off by a scant .01 percent. Eerily accurate.

But it mattered not a whit that we predicted what was likely going to happen. What really mattered was the fact that accurate models and lists for different voter groups meant that the volunteers were using your time efficiently and effectively—again, talking to the right voters about the right things at the right time.

Right about now you're probably wondering about 2016, when even the Trump campaign's models predicted a convincing Clinton victory, with less than a 20 percent chance of winning. Its leadership held briefings with the national media on Election Day, explaining before the polls closed why they had lost.

So the models were off, but here's the surprise: they were not off by much. The killer was that the discrepancies just happened to be (1) on the margins and (2) in the most crucial swing (that is, battleground) states. So (3) pretty much all the mistakes broke against Clinton. Three strikes, and you know what happens next.

Overall, the Clinton and Trump campaigns had made smart, data- and model-informed decisions about whom to target for persuasion and GOTV. It's likely that Clinton's models were too confident about the turnout from some younger voters and African American voters, core members of the Obama coalition that she inherited. And they overestimated support levels in rural and exurban areas, losing counties 70 to 30 that they thought would be 60 to 40 or even 50–50. If they had known this at the time, the Clinton campaign could have increased contact with some of those younger and African American voters in the upper Midwest, and with more urgency. They also could have invested in more persuasion work with rural and exurban voter targets.

The lesson: we can't rely just on the models, and we can't blame the models. We also have to have campaign strategies in place that address all likely scenarios. In 2020, it would be nice if the final models show Trump with a 0 percent chance of winning. That's not going to be the case. To win, our GOTV operation, utterly dependent on volunteers, will need to start with a deadly accurate sense of which voters the campaign and the volunteers should concentrate on, and then be deadly efficient in carrying out the operation.

Early voting is important. The campaign will work hard to nail down as many of these early votes as possible, thus leaving more resources available for Election Day. Now, I know that some people enjoy the excitement and camaraderie of voting on Election Day. Traveling to your precinct polling location; standing in line with your neighbors and fellow citizens; bringing your children with you into the voting booth; making your choices; turning in your paper ballot or getting a receipt from the machine; getting that important "I voted" merit badge; leaving the school, church, community center, or someone's garage.

That's right, in San Francisco, where I live now, many official polling stations are in someone's garage.

It can give you a great overall feeling that you exercised your franchise in and surrounded by your community. If you feel super strongly about that experience, and your life will be poorer for not having done it, by all means enjoy the Election Day ritual.

If you feel less strongly about the experience and live in a state that has no-excuse early voting (meaning you want to vote early or absentee), you can just do it, there doesn't have to be a reason or need. I implore you to make plans to vote early. Apply for an absentee ballot or plan to vote early in person at an early voting site. Some states, like California, allow you to become a permanent vote-by-mail citizen. Like clockwork, your ballot comes in the mail in the weeks prior to Election Day.

Some states, sadly, require an excuse or reason to vote early by absentee—a health challenge, you will be out of town for work, you have no way of getting to the polls. It's real retrograde stuff. Check your local rules online.

For the majority of you who can vote early or by email unrestrictedly, apply common sense. Something unanticipated could come up—a work crisis, transportation issue, family caregiving, or illness. Why risk losing your own vote? For those of you who plan to be active in the campaign on Election Day, you want to be free and clear of anything that could cannibalize your volunteer time. Driving to your local school to vote, waiting in line, filling in your ballot, then driving back to a phone bank or canvass staging area could take an hour. That's a bunch of GOTV target voters you won't be talking to. And if thousands of other volunteers also take time away from their volunteer shifts to vote, all of a sudden we are talking about large numbers of voters who may need a reminder, a prod, or a ride but won't get it. This would be a tragedy.

Please, get your vote against Donald Trump in the bank, safely, securely, and on your own schedule, if you can do so legally. This is important no matter where you live. We need your vote to help Democrats up and down the ticket, and while the presidential race in your state may not be close, your local U.S. House race, state senate race, or state rep race could be decided on the margins.

You should be encouraging everyone in your circle to vote early as well. The same cautionary notes apply for them. In this world, complications abound. So persuade your friends and family and fellow supporters of our nominee to bank their votes. Keep a list so you can check them off and of course ensure that you are signing them up to help with voter turnout efforts in the weeks leading up to and on Election Day.

Maybe these admonitions sound obsessive, but obsessive is what we need to be in 2020.

Our nominee's campaign will be laser focused on maximizing early vote, both in terms of banking votes early and freeing up as many people as possible for Election Day duties, be it GOTV volunteering, canvassing key target neighborhoods in Philly, or calling into Milwaukee from your home in Oklahoma City.

As I mentioned, the campaigns can track who has voted early in person or mailed in a ballot. The raw numbers—votes in so far—are not that valuable. What is valuable is the makeup of that early voting cohort. In each case, the campaign doesn't know how these diligent citizens voted, but it does know their respective "support" and "turnout" scores on the 1 to 100 scale, which allow the campaign to estimate what share of the early voters it is probably picking up (that is, if they have high support numbers) and what share it needs to pick up in the rest of the early voting period and on Election Day.

What it really hopes to see is a lot of voters whose "support" number is good, but whose "turnout" number is not so good—first-time voters, young voters, voters who do not regularly vote, voters who have not voted recently. As the campaign creates and executes early vote plans, and monitors its progress, it will focus closely on these people. It is of the highest imperative to get their votes in the bank early because otherwise they may never be deposited at all.

If the campaign isn't happy with the early numbers and believes it is on a trajectory to fall short in a precinct, county, state—or any combination—it may devote more resources to try to goose up the numbers, especially with the critical probably-for-us-but-may-not-vote targets. The Trump campaign will also be laser focused on the early voters. For political insiders, this campaign within the campaign is fascinating. For you—volunteers, supporters of the Democrats' nominee—it's more than that. We have to win it. In some jurisdictions, more than half of all votes will come in early.

So Election Day, mercifully, is here. We've endured it all: polls, debates, social media posts and stats, ads, hourly money solicitations, pundit predictions. We have finally arrived at the day when the only thing that counts will be actual votes cast by actual voters in actual states. In states like Pennsylvania, where only a few of the votes will be cast by mail, everything rides on Election Day execution. In Colorado or Nevada, more than 50 percent of the votes will already be in. So the results in your state may or not be riding solely on Election Day turnout and execution, but as I've said quite a few times about issues that may seem important (like the inequities in the electoral college), for now, it doesn't matter. You volunteers and the staff supporting you still have to break the tape with everything you've got. A great first half can be overwhelmed by a lousy second half.

If you doubt what I'm saying, remember Florida in 2016. Looking at the early vote data heading into Election Day and also taking into account whatever wisdom the campaigns were sharing, experts on the subject (there are very few of them) thought that while Florida would always be close, you'd rather be Clinton than Trump. And losing Florida would surely be a backbreaker for Trump.

They were wrong. Why? As everyone who follows politics knows, the fundamental nationwide problem in 2016 was that all the models overestimated Clinton's share of white voters with no college education and therefore understated Trump's support in the panhandle of Florida, in Iowa, just about everywhere. Why? Trump ended up having more appeal than polls or electoral history suggested (there were some counties that flipped *40* points between 2012 and 2016), so turnout was also higher than projected in many of those counties and the models were baking in higher Clinton support goals and lower Trump margins than reality would demonstrate.

The error was most blatantly important in Wisconsin. Had the models been accurate there, the Clinton campaign could have taken countermeasures across the board, on the airwaves, and in the trenches. But thanks to the numbers suggesting it was a safe blue—never dreaming it could lose the Badger State—it hardly bothered to campaign at all.

That doesn't mean they would have won it. The Trump campaign would have responded in kind and GOP turnout could have surged even more—but I'm sure it would have felt better to go all out there.

In Florida, the error played out in one specific way, and it wasn't with early voting. While the campaign felt good about the state, a feeling affirmed by most observers, it still knew the state would be decided by a percentage point or two. In the weeks leading up to the election, the campaign and the volunteers were pedal to the metal getting voters out early. No, the problem was Election Day itself. It was clear from the early numbers that turnout was going to surge well beyond historical levels, but in all likelihood, the Clinton campaign had enough supporters identified and modeled to win Florida. Their GOTV "universe" was large enough. In fact, their actual vote total in Florida turned out to be higher than Obama's winning number had been four years earlier against Mitt Romney.

But this still wasn't high enough, which must have seemed incredibly frustrating to someone who produced the most votes in Florida a Democratic candidate for president had ever received. The strength of the Republican turnout on Election Day shocked the pros. Trump turned out just about everyone he could have.

Florida in 2016 is a great and painful example of how critical the intensity of your supporters is, how critical GOTV is for any Democratic presidential candidate. In 2020, we have to generate this intensity as early as possible, and we've got to maintain it until the last voter walks out of the last booth of the last battleground state. I'll say it again: we Democrats always leave more votes on the table than the Republicans. Our job in 2020 is to help ensure that we minimize those numbers so that no matter what the turnout, we can win. Of course we don't know yet what the exact turnout will be in 2020, but we know it will be high. We better assume *super* high, and plan accordingly.

So what is your personal GOTV strategy? Well, first, make certain that anybody in your circle who has somehow dodged all your pesky efforts to get them to vote early does finally vote on November 3. Don't take no for an answer. Make sure they know about the 537 votes that lost Florida in 2000. Imagine what it would be like to lose to Trump by the same kind of margin. Triple the pain, at least.

If you live in a state that doesn't allow early voting just for the sake of convenience, be sure you provoke and prod to make sure everyone has a plan for voting on Election Day, has made arrangements vis-à-vis work, family, everything. Do they know where their polling location is? Yes, because you've told them earlier. How they are going to get there? What time? Do they need help with child or elder care? Can they manage a long line (don't get me started on how outrageous that is) or will they have to leave and go back to work or home? If so, they need a plan to account for that. The folks you are badgering may become annoyed, but they'll forgive you, don't worry. They know you're coming from the right place. And their annoyance will actually help, because it might bring into the conversation questions and complications that need airing. We have to treat every supporter of our nominee as a precious, fragile egg. Everywhere. We want the map to be as blue as possible on election night. Get that egg in the bank!

Volunteers in the campaign's ongoing GOTV efforts will have a variety of ways to reach out to voters outside of your circle. If you live in a battleground state or choose to travel to one, you are in for a special and unique experience. Canvassing when the stakes are so high is a remarkable experience. You will see people driving their cars to run errands, kids riding their bikes to playgrounds, fans watching basketball at local watering holes—people going about their everyday activities. You are also walking the very streets that will determine who our next president is. You will have in your grasp the very names of those voters who are key to the election in that community, that state, and our country.

Assuming the campaign has done its job well, your list will include only voters still in play for us. They are registered, they have not voted yet, and they are not planning to vote for Donald Trump. The campaign's data experts believe these people are solid for the Democrat if they vote, but they may not. If enough of them decide to take a pass, we will end up with a repeat of the horrors in Wisconsin and Michigan in 2016—losses that could have been prevented if we had produced just the expected, not even exceptional, turnout in Democratic base areas.

As always with canvassing, a lot of people won't be home. You'll be supplied with door hangers from the campaign—like those that pizza restaurants have—reminding the voter to vote, informing them where to vote, and closing with some motivating message. This is good, but more motivational will be your personal note on the door hanger, expressing in your own words how much their vote will mean.

You should put the note in your own words, but here are a few examples left with the door hanger for, let's say,

Veronica in Dane County, Wisconsin, the weekend before the election.

"Veronica, sorry to miss you. Your vote could make the difference in Wisconsin! We need you on Tuesday."

"Veronica, sorry to miss you. My name is Michelle and I'm supporting [name of our candidate] because my daughter needs health care and Trump may take it away. Please vote on Tuesday for all our kids!"

Or more simply, "We can't afford 4 more years of Trump. We need you Veronica!"

Whatever moves you, because when Veronica returns home and reads your note, she may be moved as well. Not by the campaign slogans and pictures but by your personal appeal.

When people do answer the door, you will likely hear a variety of responses. The most common may be a slightly exasperated, "I'm voting! I've told everyone's who asked." The simple reply will suffice: "Thanks for your vote. It'll all be over Tuesday and we can celebrate both the election being over and Trump's loss."

But some may say, "I'm voting but not for your candidate. Both parties are crooked, I'm sending a message by voting for Smith, he seems pretty good, or maybe Robinson, she seems pretty good too." Smith and Robinson are third-party candidates. We've already discussed some ideas for engaging and hopefully converting these "flight-risk" voters, as we sometimes call them.

If you've been active in the campaign, you've almost certainly had these conversations. But now you find yourself in your own urgent crisis: at this late hour, a voter in a key battleground state is saying they are definitely voting, but not for your candidate. As I've explained, this is exactly how Trump gets his "win number" down, by having just enough #NeverTrump voters go the third-party route.

If you feel as passionately about electing a new president as I hope you do, you may feel this is one of the most important conversations of your life. As always, you'll be understanding, not critical, much less dismissive. You may find a connection on an issue; you may even share his distaste for the two-party system.

But on the eve of the election, it's important that you try to get these voters to focus on this fact: if just a few voters in the state choose a third party, it could flip the election to Trump. Be specific and make it personal. Do they really want eight years of Trump instead of four? If not, the only vote to ensure he is a disgraced one-term loser is for the Democratic nominee.

Or you could hear at the door that your target voter is simply not going to vote. It won't matter who wins, so what's the point? Crisis, again. An issue may be your way in. See if you can casually talk your way to one the voter deeply cares about, say, public transportation, and make the case that our nominee, unlike the incumbent, will press for more funding and support new public transportation projects and rebuilding those that are decaying. Or maybe the issue is Social Security— probably a top concern for older voters. You can state unequivocally that because Trump cut taxes so deeply for the top 1 percent, in his second term he is going to have to join the Republicans in Congress who have long wanted to slash Social Security. The Democratic candidate will try to roll back the tax cuts for the rich and protect Social Security.

Maybe the best way forward in this case is the simple, unthreatening reminder that our candidate doesn't have to be the second coming of Lincoln or Roosevelt. We hope the Democrat will make some great stuff happen, but we know he or she will stop some really terrible stuff from happening. We can't expect all of our voters to cast their ballots with stars in their eyes, wearing our candidate's swag, sermonizing and singing praises to all who will listen.

Holding your nose and voting counts as much in the final tally as casting your vote with unbridled enthusiasm. Figure out how to get this reluctant voter to cast a reluctant vote. Your conversation on the porch is probably the campaign's best opportunity with this voter. If you don't succeed in this exchange, it's highly likely that this potential vote will go down the drain. Not to put any pressure on you or anything.

Or you may hear, "I don't think I'll have time. I'll try but with school and work, I can't afford to wait in line. It's always so long."

Long lines—that's a common refrain with our disgraceful system, but you can't snap your fingers and fix it. This seems to be the last arena in America where we are not trying to optimize efficiency. Why don't we use data and modeling to determine how many people will be voting at certain polling locations, so we know how much equipment will be needed to minimize the line, and when the busiest times will be so you can surge enough poll workers to meet the demand?

It is such an insanely simple problem to solve, but I believe we know the answer. Long lines mean some voters will have to leave without voting, which is exactly what many Republicans want to see in certain minority and working-class neighborhoods, where people get paid by the hour, not in salary or stock options. Republicans will never work to correct the flaws, and they fight every effort by Democrats to right this wrong. But there's no excuse for the confusion in jurisdictions in which Democrats run the elections. The lines happen in plenty of places where we call the shots.

Embrace data, optimize for a great user experience with short lines. There are many problems we wrestle with that have hard or nonexistent solutions. This is not one of them. Every Democratic mayor and Governor should be on top of this, demanding and driving their teams to run tighter election days.

End of diatribe. Back to our busy voter who doesn't have the time for long lines. You might be able to help solve this problem. Perhaps if she had a ride to the polls from her workplace, then another one back to her community college. Presto! An hour of sitting in the subway cut out of her busy day.

On Election Day, the national campaign, perhaps as well as your local Democratic Party and/or some progressive organizations, will have ride-to-the-polls programs in place. If so, they will have been explained to you before you hit the doors. Providing rides is a critical GOTV activity on Election Day. In this instance of the voter worried that the long lines would bust her tight schedule for the day, take personal charge. Be creative. You can get this new friend to the polls. The more time and interest you invest in her—not her vote, *her*—the more motivated she becomes.

Some people simply can't get to the polls, period, on their own accord. They want to vote for our nominee, perhaps even enthusiastically so. They'll be home on

Election Day, but because of health, age, or family obligations where they can't leave home easily, they just can't
get to the polls and they didn't vote early. This can be one
of the most urgent, occasionally panic-inducing exchanges
you'll have. Here is a voter who needs no convincing. Easy,
guaranteed vote. But the deposit may not happen. It
will happen only because the ride-to-the-polls operation
is running smoothly. Robot cars are not the answer, yet.
We need enough human beings behind enough steering
wheels.

I urge you to consider being one of the drivers. It's
easy to sign up through our nominee's website. I've driven
a few times through the years, and there are few experiences as satisfying as picking up someone who, otherwise,
wouldn't have been able to exercise his sacred right to
vote. Driver and passenger generally have a great conversation. Both of you sincerely appreciate the other's contribution to our democracy. You know and see the direct
impact of your work as clearly as with any other activity
in an election—depositing a new friend at the polls
who is going to vote for your candidate. You watch him
walk inside the library, you watch him exit and return to
your car, a vote in the bank.

Campaigns also may utilize ride-sharing services
like Uber or Lyft, ordering rides to the polls with a
press of a button. Or these companies may partner with

nonprofits committed to voter participation, providing rides at no expense to campaigns. But the personal experience, for both the volunteer driver and the voter, is far more effective and meaningful than the third-party option.

If you come across a voter on your canvassing shift who will need a ride, and you live in the neighborhood, why not take matters into your own hands and offer then and there to come back and do the honors yourself? Wouldn't that be downright awesome? No good reason to wait for the campaign apparatus, dependable though it is. After this voter has shared with you his or her barrier to voting, you will be the friendly and helpful face coming back to make sure they can participate fully in their democracy and in choosing their next commander in chief. Maybe this will be in-person early voting, maybe on Election Day. Doesn't matter. Exchange mobile phone info and establish the best time, then text a reminder the morning of.

Create your own ride-to-the-polls caravan. Drive multiple voters to the polls. Just be sure to space them out timewise and factor in traffic. You can't run late with any of them. Letting those dominoes start falling the wrong way would be a disaster.

Whatever you do for our candidate's cause in the general election and whenever you do it, I urge you to include GOTV activities as part of your mix. This is where the rubber meets the road. As we've seen many times, the whole point of all the other activities is to ensure that we match our higher "support" levels with actual turnout. We need you in the field to make sure we reach every human being possible. GOTV will also be some of the most rewarding and tangible work you do. It is as real as it gets. You are encouraging, enabling, and securing actual votes. Not tweets, posts, polls, or punditry. The real thing.

And remember that one of our two major political parties, almost universally so, acts as if its representatives have taken a sworn oath to make it harder for young voters and voters of color to vote. And we have a president who on close to a daily basis cries about voter fraud that is nonexistent, has suggested that legitimate mail-in and provisional votes should not be counted, and almost certainly through his campaign will sponsor voter-suppression and "confusion" advertising. Suddenly there will be ads targeted at low-propensity Democratic voters stating wrong polling locations and times, as well as notices stating you need to bring your birth certificate and Social Security card to vote. All lies, all despicable, and all sure to happen.

And Lord knows what he'll do on Twitter heading up to Election Day. It will certainly not be to encourage participation by anyone who does not look like him.

All that bad faith should be motivation enough to help people exercise their franchise in the service of electing a president we can be proud of.

GOTV takes dead aim at the GOP's most consistent campaign strategy—to rig the system so voters who may oppose them have to work really hard to vote.

On November 3, let's make them pay for their attack on our Democracy.

9

ELECTION NIGHT

★ ★ ★

T he campaign is over, your work is concluded, why do I care where and how you take in the results on the big night? How could this be important for our only subject here—defeating Donald Trump? Well, from my earliest days in politics, I've believed there's a relationship between how you campaign and how you handle election night. You want all the positive energy you can get in the final weeks of the campaign, and now you're exhausted, but you need to keep it going for six more hours. Maybe that energy mysteriously flows both ways. That's all I'm saying, even if you're now picturing me as the guy wearing a tinfoil hat.

And what has been the source of this energy? People. The campaign has been about your fellow citizens—staffers, volunteers, voters, potential voters, potential supporters—lots of people. For the deeply invested, it has been a rich education in human nature. I strongly suggest you make election night also about people—specifically, the ones you've worked with so hard. If you have spent the whole of Election Day driving voters back and forth to the polls, or if you've traveled to a battleground state, or you're working at a phone bank wherever you live, you should strongly consider gathering with your fellow volunteers, whether at a local campaign office, a hotel ballroom where an "official" party is happening, a local bar, or at one of the volunteer's houses.

If you haven't been out volunteering on Election Day, you'd better have a damn good reason—like, a really, really compelling reason—why you couldn't find at least an hour to make GOTV calls from your home.

You come from different backgrounds, education, jobs, income, family situations, age, race, genders, sexual orientations, and political volunteering experiences—the ultimate Rainbow Coalition. You have the shared experience of knowing how hard it was to find the time to give to the campaign; the rude people who hung up when you called them; the doors slammed but also the doors opened to wonderful conversation and commitment; the funny stories about the funny people you encountered; the days you thought for sure we were going to win and the days you were convinced of the opposite. But you share one thing in common: making Donald Trump a one-term president is one of the most important desires of your lives. And you have banded together, a disparate group of people becoming a powerfully united citizen army. You deserve to share this night with your campaign compadres who have also laid it all on the line.

It's just a tremendous experience to share these moments as the returns roll in, states are called, and the electoral college map fills. When a key state is super close, way too close for comfort, after 80 percent of the vote is in, having some people on hand with whom you can talk this through, who may have found a Twitter feed that analyzes the vote that is left to be counted in that state and suggests we are likely to win—isn't that better than fretting and rooting around the internet on your own? When the powers that be then call Pennsylvania for our nominee, and it returns to its rightful blue color on the big electoral map, won't it be more fun and meaningful to hug, high-five, and yell "Yes!" at the top of your lungs with others who feel the same elation?

When the TV coverage cuts to a quiet and concerned Trump election-night party at one of his god-awful hotel ballrooms after Michigan is called for our nominee, don't you want to laugh, cheer, and take in that amazingly beautiful scene with others? And for the coup de grâce, Trump's concession speech, or lack of one?

If for some reason a gathering of your fellow volunteers isn't in the cards, think carefully where you want to be, and with whom. Alone? With a group? Small or large? Friends and family? Certainly give this as much thought as how you would plan to watch the Super Bowl or the Oscars. I'd vote for any of the above except being alone. Alone is no good. It's the wrong energy—completely in defiance of your campaigning life. You'll want the culmination of all that work to exactly suit your purposes and hopefully create the perfect memory of the night America began to erase the stain of the Trump interregnum.

If you're with the family and you have kids who were old enough to be traumatized by Trump's election and all that has come since, make sure they have some friends with them as well. They'll give you a furtive hug or a high five, but sharing and celebrating a return to the America they want to grow up in and will soon enough eventually contribute to and lead will be most meaningful with people of their own age, both the memories that are created and the conversations they will have.

After all, they are the most important factor in this election. We want to win for them and their future above all else. Make sure you include them, talk to them about how they want to witness election night and its history. Hopefully they've also been engaged in the election in the ways they can, joining you to volunteer at the local campaign office, traveling to battleground states, following and discussing the election twists and turns with you throughout the summer and fall. Make election night a great capstone for them.

On the other hand, family can be dicey. I say this from personal experience. With two exceptions, I have spent every election in my working life either in the boiler room, talking to the camera on network coverage, or somewhere out in a state where I'd been working on an election. The first exception was in 2004, John Kerry's race to send W back to the ranch. This was two months after my son was born, and my wife and I huddled together in Washington after I'd spent much of those two months on the road working on the dozen campaign projects my firm was handling. We were really happy to be settling in for the night together. I was going to be off the road now—the new normal postelection—and then the first exit polls suggested that John Kerry would actually pull off this very close race.

As is often the case, the exits were off. Way off. So that first family night ended up being a huge bummer.

The other time, my wife and I invited friends over to

our place (in San Francisco, where we now live) on November 8, 2016, and prepared to celebrate the election of our first woman president. Tears flowed instead of champagne, hangdog faces instead of high fives. This is why I say family-oriented election nights haven't worked out so well for the Morgan-Plouffes. We'll have to think long and hard about November 3, 2020. We'll be mixing things up.

I've always been superstitious about elections. David Axelrod, Robert Gibbs, and I all wore the same ties on election night 2012 that we wore in 2008; I think I wore the same suit. In 2016, we had ordered food from a BBQ place in San Francisco. I've never been back there again, and I never will, and I'll never have anything even related to barbecue on any election night ever again. If you are the least bit superstitious, please don't do anything in 2020 that you did the night Trump won. Do the opposite. What's the opposite of barbecue? That's one of the issues I'll be determining in the months ahead.

You don't think any of this could possibly matter? My answer: what if you're wrong? Leave no stone unturned. That has been the ruling mantra in your campaigning life for a long time. Carry it forward one more night. Find a superstition and indulge it. Humor me, if nothing else. I certainly will need all the good vibes possible on November 3.

Next question: How do you want to follow the results? There are so many more options than there used to be—the internet, apps, social media, and probably newer categories I've never heard of. What do you watch out for? How do you handle expectations? How have you developed those expectation over the preceding weeks? You'll have the polls, what the predictive modeling experts are saying, your own gut. Healthiest to kind of ignore it all and assume the odds are 50-50. This approach should keep you working hard and best prepared for any outcome on election night.

I grew up watching the results come in on network television, and this is still how I envision election night. It's how the majority of Americans spend the evening. Sure, the commentators can be annoying, and they never seem to remember basic things (early Virginia results will skew heavily Republican, for example), but they're still what counts for most people. Even for us with both Obama campaigns, even though we knew pretty early, based on our internal evaluation of the actual vote count, that we had won both elections, it wasn't quite "real" until the networks made it official and declared Barack Obama the president-elect and then declared his reelection as president.

In our media-soaked environment, the standing of

the networks is necessarily diminished, but their calls in a presidential election are still a defining moment in our shared American experience. Even the one time they got it wrong, in 2000.

If the networks' old-fashioned election-night coverage is your jam, which one do you want to watch? A lot can factor into that decision—preference for the anchors' and analysts' talent, the graphics, maybe even the music (on this last count I'm partial to NBC's accompaniment and hope they don't change it for 2020). Some people like to flip around among the stations. Be my guest, but there is something about turning on the set at 7 or 8 p.m. Eastern Standard Time and keeping it on the same station all the way until the bitter end. This is a calmer experience and you can follow consistent commentary about the status of the returns, trends in battleground states, analysis of the exit polls. The one exception to staying on one network the entire night is if our nominee is declared the winner, then I'd suggest dropping whatever other station you are watching and flip over to Fox. Watching them deal with declaring that their central product and moneymaker has lost the White House may, by itself, make all the hard work you put in during the election worth it.

If the networks are not your jam, if you're interested in looking at the returns in more detail than they can offer

on the air, many news sites such as nytimes.com, cnn
.com, and washingtonpost.com give you both the broad-
brush overview and maps that link all the way "down" to
the county level. This is important information to aug-
ment the networks' data that, for example, 50 percent
of the precincts have reported in a given state. Which
precincts?! This makes all the difference. Perhaps that 50
percent is a fairly representative sampling in terms of
demographics and past voting results—a solid mixture of
traditionally blue, red, and purple precincts—and therefore is a good clue about the direction the election is taking in the state.

But often the outstanding precincts skew one way or
the other.

I noted previously that the early Virginia results will
skew heavily Republican, as the more rural parts of the
state post results before now heavily Democratic northern
Virginia. The same discrepancy often happens in Ohio.
In those two states, our nominee's standing will strengthen
considerably as the rest of the precincts report. The opposite may be the case in Pennsylvania, where it's the
smaller, redder counties that come in later. Then of course
there is Florida, which always seems to be close from the
moment that first results are posted to the bitter end.

A combination of sources works well. Perhaps you
prefer having the analysis and map clicking done for you

by skilled analysts like John King on CNN or Chuck Todd on NBC. But if you live in a key battleground state or simply want to follow them closely, I highly recommend having a computer or iPad open so you can scroll the site of your choosing. It's a more active and engaged way to watch the numbers roll in that will determine both our next president and our future.

Many of you will spend time on sites with data experts such as Nate Silver's blog, *FiveThirtyEight*, Nate Cohn with the *New York Times*'s *The Upshot*, or Dave Wasserman with the *Cook Political Report*. In the weeks leading up to the election, these sources will average all the polls in the battleground states as well as factor in other historical election data and offer a new prediction each day for the percentage chance each candidate has to win each state and the overall election. Those sites are fun, and on average, they are more right than wrong but of course far from perfect. If you are not careful, they can also drive you crazy, if not induce a state of outright paralysis. Check one or more once a day, if you must, but don't refresh every fifteen minutes and certainly don't waste precious time fretting or bed-wetting. Stay focused on the task at hand.

Some of you will remember the *New York Times* election meter from 2016, part of *The Upshot* coverage. Before the returns started coming in on election night, based on all the polls and other data, the needle registered a more than 80 percent likelihood that Clinton would win the presidency. As actual state returns started to come in, the needle began to oh so slowly drift to the right, the Florida numbers pushed the needle farther, and then as we started to get enough raw vote from Wisconsin, Michigan, and Pennsylvania, Clinton became the smallest of favorites. At some point, the needle favored Trump slightly, for the first time. It was like watching the proverbial car crash in slow motion.

If you were following that needle, that was a moment you will not soon forget. And then the needle kept slowly but apparently inexorably moving into the red, favoring Trump more and more strongly. Clinton's path to victory was narrowing precipitously.

That needle captured the election-night emotions perfectly: early confidence . . . a little unease . . . a little more unease . . . not going to be a blowout . . . but she'll still win . . . the terrible realization that it's now a jump ball . . . followed too quickly by the horror of understanding it would now take a miracle to keep Trump out of the White House. Then the needle was at 100 percent, and it was accurate. Donald Trump would be our next president.

For the congressional elections in 2018, the needle was accurate again on many races and overall House and

Senate control. It will probably be pretty accurate in 2020 too, but I would not recommend staring straight at it for five or six hours. Include the needle as part of your potpourri of election-night inputs. Mix up your sensory inputs and sources of information.

On the social media front, there are an infinite number of choices, folks who will be interpreting the results in real time, and some of these sources actually know what they're writing about. Jon Ralston, @ralstonreports, is a journalist in Nevada who knows the numbers in his state cold. Steve Schale, @steveschale, in Florida helped Obama win the state twice but looks at the numbers in a clinically nonpartisan way as they come in. In each state, there will be local political science professors, journalists, and operatives who will add experience, context, and value to your election night.

You have probably noted that I've emphasized the positive in this little chapter, even though we all know it's quite possible that the incumbent could win. If we don't get right all that each of us can do, he probably will. This possibility has been my entire emphasis for the preceding pages. Election night is fun to think about— my images of the celebration are blissful, I can tell you— and I do believe that the positive-energy circuits between that night and the campaign can work in our favor—but what I really believe is that now it's time to set the daydreams aside and get back to work.

Election Day will be here before you know it—there's literally not a day—or hour—to waste.

Let's go win this thing.

Acknowledgments

When I first raised writing this book, and then added a young reader's version to the mix, my family did not blink. They were all in, enthusiastically, and gave great ideas and advice. That kept me motivated to push through and try and do my best work, but most importantly to try and make a meaningful difference, which was and is our North Star.

I hope we have done that with this book, but even more important than that to me is that Olivia, Everett, and Vivian are proud of it and that as a family we live out the ideas and lessons laid out here in 2020 and beyond.

When I first broached the idea of this book with David Larabell, my agent at CAA, his instinct was clear and true—if at all possible I should work with Wendy Wolf and Viking, who published my first book more than ten years ago. Don't talk to anyone else, this would be the right home for *Citizen's Guide*.

He was right and once again I was reminded of Wendy's clarity, firmness (even when not entirely welcomed at first), judgment, loyalty, and belief in her authors and their projects.

So thanks to Wendy, and Mike Bryan, who had some great thoughts on content and structure that are reflected in the final product.

Thanks to the whole team at Viking, from the editors to the marketing and PR whizzes and all the staff who made this book a reality.

This book is for and inspired by the millions and millions of Americans who fight for change and progress, in ways large and small, each and every day. You give me hope on the darkest days and confidence that, as Dr King said, The arc of the moral universe is long, but it bends towards justice.

1127

2/2355